ALERT!

ALERTA!

ALERTA!

SNAPSHOTS OF EUROPE'S ANTI-FASCIST STRUGGLE

ALERTA!

PATRICK STRICKLAND

AK PRESS

Alerta! Alerta!: Snapshots of Europe's Anti-Fascist Struggle

© 2018 Patrick Strickland

This edition © 2018 AK Press (Chico, Edinburgh)

ISBN 978-1-84935-330-4

E-ISBN 978-1-84935-331-1

Library of Congress Control Number: 2018932266

AK Press	AK Press
370 Ryan Ave. #100	33 Tower St.
Chico, CA 95973	Edinburgh EH6 7BN
United States	Scotland
www.akpress.org	www.akuk.com
akpress@akpress.org	ak@akedin.demon.co.uk

The above addresses would be delighted to provide you with the latest AK Press distribution catalog, which features books, pamphlets, zines, and stylish apparel published and/or distributed by AK Press. Alternatively, visit our websites for the complete catalog, latest news, and secure ordering.

Cover and interior design by Quemadura

Photographs by Patrick Strickland

Printed in the USA

When I first set out to write *Alerta! Alerta!*, I had little idea of how to go about writing a book. Yet, after years of working as a reporter in the Middle East, North Africa, Europe, and North America, I had built a series of important relationships with friends, colleagues, and comrades far more intelligent than me.

This book would not have been possible without those people or the ones who came before them. Without the journalistic support, friendship, and help of Dylan Collins, whom I first met in Palestine in 2012, I certainly would not have grown into the reporter, writer, and person I am now.

Creede Newton, whom I met in 2009 while an undergraduate at the University of North Texas, has always been available for feedback, help, and assistance.

Laurin-Whitney Gottbrath and Anealla Safdar, both colleagues and close friends of mine at *Al Jazeera English*, were boundless sources of inspiration both professionally and personally. Their company was irreplaceable, whether in the office or during late nights at Boston's in Doha.

Long before I became a journalist, my friend Sarah Jones, whom I also met during my undergraduate studies, inspired me to focus my life on writing. Our discussions on literature remain with me until today.

The love and support of Kyle Irion and Derek Brozowski cannot go unmentioned. Both helped me develop my worldview. Most im-

ACKNOWLEDGMENTS

X

portantly, their acute empathy has had a lifelong impact. Without them, I never would have become a journalist or author.

My mother, Tracy, has always been a source of love, support, and encouragement. She worked nights at a neighborhood bar to raise my brother and me, and without her tireless efforts I would not have developed the politics or work ethic that were requisite to writing this book. My stepfather Eric and brother Pierce have been pillars in my life, including throughout the writing of this book.

In Greece, the help of Nick Paleologos was indispensable. In Italy, the work of my fixer, Alessandra Pugliese, made the completion of that chapter possible. In Germany, I relied on my dear friend and colleague Natalija Miletic, for whom I am eternally grateful. In Slovakia, Jana Čavojská worked endlessly and tracked down activists, politicians, and others. In Croatia, Ladislav Tomić and Jerko Bakotin made my research and reporting possible.

Nancy Stockdale, my undergraduate history professor and closest friend, opened my mind to the world. Without her, I never would have taken the step to move abroad and seek a different life.

Nada Homsi, for whom my respect is immeasurable, has always read over my notes and stories, many of which have found their way into this book.

Without the editors with whom I had close relationships, among them Ali Abunimah and Maureen Murphy at the *Electronic Intifada*, I would not have learned the basics of journalism.

ACKNOWLEDGMENTS

My editors at AK Press worked long hours to make *Alerta! Alerta!* a reality. I am unable to adequately express my appreciation for all their work.

I remain indebted to many people whose names are not listed here. Nonetheless, I am grateful for everyone who has helped and supported me along the way.

Finally, any acknowledgment would be incomplete without expressing my deepest gratitude to everyone I interviewed for this book.

ACKNOWLEDGMENTS

MEN OF GOD AND MEN OF WAR
HAVE STRANGE AFFINITIES.

—Cormac McCarthy, *Blood Meridian,*
or the Evening Redness in the West

HOW THE U.S. MEDIA DISCOVERED
ANTI-FASCISM—ALMOST ONE HUNDRED
YEARS LATE

Anti-fascism is growing, whether in my home state of Texas in the United States or on the streets of Athens, Greece, where activists are taking sledgehammers to the windows of the neo-Nazi Golden Dawn party's headquarters. Whether they were shutting down a racist speaker or protesting a news program for providing racists an unchecked platform, anti-fascists made their presence unavoidable in 2017, the year I set out to write this book.

Arguing that anti-fascists are successful may seem absurd. At present, far-right political parties across Europe often have access to the corridors of power, even if their rise is often exaggerated—or worse, fueled—by the media coverage these groups garner.

The developments taking place since the November 2016 election of Donald Trump in the United States have thrown that country into turmoil, and anti-fascism has taken root both there and in Europe. While this book will be focused on Europe and based on my reporting in several countries across the European Union, the debates that have emerged about anti-fascism are informative on a more general level. Mainstream media outlets and professional pundits have—with rare exceptions—painted anti-fascists as little more than a reaction to the white supremacy and white nationalism into which Trump breathed life throughout his campaign and since his election.

Antifa, as anti-fascists are known in colloquial parlance, are sometimes depicted as almost tantamount to the very fascists whom they fight against. They are the "extreme left," according to popular public opinion, and their commitment to direct confrontation and shutting down public appearances by far-right figures renders them opponents of free speech. Commentators in mainstream news outlets paint a grim picture of two extreme poles, the neo-Nazis and their opponents, leaving audiences to believe that the liberal center is the last reasonable and democratic political space to occupy. This interpretation of recent history is a false dichotomy. Antifa's alleged disregard for free speech, we are told, is what makes them "the real fascists," if you subscribe to the worldview of the right-wing Breitbart News Network that has become a mouthpiece for the Trump regime.

Yet the sheer growth of anti-fascist groups in these turbulent times is a victory of sorts. A highly active and visible Antifa organization in my hometown of Dallas—no bastion for leftist or antiauthoritarian politics—would have been unthinkable five years ago. Nonetheless, it is a reality today. While there has been an upsurge in media interest in the resurgent anti-fascist movement, it has not translated into positive or accurate coverage—with very few exceptions. The local affiliate of NBC covered a recent Antifa action in Richardson, situated just outside Dallas. The Bureau of American Islamic Relations (BAIR), a virulently right-wing group steeped in Islamophobia, planned and staged a pro-test outside the Islamic Association of North Texas in March 2017. BAIR had already made a name for itself by toting rifles to local mosques and intimidating worshipers. But when the Dallas Workers Front, an anti-fascist outfit, showed up with pipes and guns to ensure the Islamic Association's safety, they were treated as radicals—always a pejorative term in liberal jargon—who merely sought a confrontation.

According to NBC's local affiliate, the Dallas Workers Front "hijacked" the counterprotest and "hurled insults" at the Islamophobic BAIR group. The Islamic Association requested that they "back off" and allow BAIR to exercise its supposed right to free speech. "When that didn't work, the two opposing sides [BAIR and the Islamic Association] unexpectedly left the rowdy group behind and decided to share lunch together," the report said.

That wasn't the case at the University of California, Berkeley, where a month earlier Antifa activists banged up a campus building and set fires, forcing the police to evacuate Milo Yiannopoulos, former Breitbart editor and right-wing media darling, before his speech was delivered. Yiannopoulos was later hosted on news programs and talk shows across the country, and Antifa was blamed for spurring yet more interest in the far-right provocateur. Credible reports suggest he intended to expose undocumented students, but that was rarely mentioned—at best, it was presented as passing context.

When a black-clad demonstrator in Washington, D.C., threw an elbow into the doughy face of white supremacist and alt-right leader Richard Spencer during Trump's inauguration in January 2017, Antifa was said to be a violent group incapable of tolerating differing views or presenting more convincing arguments against hate speech.

History will be the judge of these analyses in the U.S. context. But a sober look at the rich tradition of anti-fascism in Europe has a great deal to say about the need for confronting, fighting, and ultimately stopping the spread of fascism in all its forms.

As in the United States, the rise of the far right in Europe poses a threat to people of color, religious minorities, ethnic minorities, migrants, refugees, and political opponents. In many ways, the surge of far-right parties and groups in Europe predated the rise of Trump and his particular brand of racism and white nationalism.[1] In 2010, Hungary's Viktor Orbán was elected as prime minister for a second time after eight years of leading the opposition. In 2015, around the time that Trump was clamoring for the construction of an antimigrant wall on the U.S.-Mexico border, Orbán ordered the erection of an ominous, barbwire fence on the Hungarian–Serbian border. Orbán, who fashioned himself a defender of "Christian Europe," was comfortably reelected in April 2018.[2]

Elsewhere in Europe, the fascist threat entailed more overt displays of street violence. On Greek islands in the Aegean Sea, such as Chios, xenophobic violence was already part of daily life for refugees and their supporters. On June 6, 2016, a known supporter of the neo-Nazi Golden Dawn party slugged a fifteen-year-old Syrian boy in the face.[3] When Yannis Koutsodonotis, a fifty-year-old Greek Ministry of Health employee, attempted to inter-vene, the man tackled and pummeled him. That was nothing new in Greece, where the Golden Dawn first entered the parliament in 2012 after campaigning on the promise of escalating anti-migrant bloodshed. Self-described as "social nationalists," the Golden Dawn boasted of more than a decade of intense violence targeting refugees, migrants, minorities, leftists, anarchists, and other political opponents. In some instances, the far-right party's violence included brazen murder.

In Italy, according to a report published by *BlogActiv*, neofas-cist parties CasaPound and Forza Nuova were notorious for at-tacks "against migrants, NGOs and leftist militants."[4]

These examples are just a few of many that illustrate the human impact of the reemergence of far-right ideologies such as neofascism and ultranationalism, which are rooted in a much more distant history of European fascism. In Germany, the rise of Nazism led to the extermination of some two-thirds of Europe's prewar Jewish population and the systematic slaughter of sev-eral other groups, among them Roma, LGBTQI communities, Je-hovah's Witnesses, people with disabilities, and communists, among others.

Over the decades following the defeat of fascist regimes and their collaborators at the end of the Second World War, neofas-cism ebbed and flowed. At times more powerful and widespread than during other periods, racism and xenophobia were always cornerstones of neofascism, and violence was always its nucleus.

AUSTRIA

In October 2017, just three months before I started writing this introduction, Austria's far-right Freedom Party (FPO) won eleven seats in the national legislative elections, putting it in a position to form a coalition government with the right-wing Austrian People's Party. They formed that coalition in December 2017.

Anti-fascists were not silent. On January 13, 2018, around twenty thousand anti-fascists flooded the streets of Vienna to voice their opposition to the FPO's inclusion in the government. Many of them held placards that declared, "Don't let Nazis govern!"[5]

It was not hyperbole. Established in 1956, the FPO was founded in the wake of the Second World War by former Nazis. The FPO's inaugural leader was Anton Reinthaller, a former Nazi functionary and member of the SS paramilitary. Much of the FPO's campaign has been focused on Euroscepticism and opposed to Muslims, refugees, and other immigrants, with the party calling for Austria to join the Visegrad Group, a bloc of eastern and central European countries fighting immigration.

The FPO's new ruling figures were true to form. Less than a month after becoming a junior coalition partner, the FPO was seeking to implement its xenophobic designs. Interior Minister Herbert Kickl, a member of the FPO, said asylum seekers should be "concentrated" in camps and special centers.[6]

XXI

INTRODUCTION

HUNGARY

As Hungary neared national elections in April 2018, Prime Minister Orbán led an insidious campaign to crack down on refugees, migrants, political opponents, and nonprofit organizations, particularly those that work with asylum seekers.

On Sunday, February 18, 2018, Orbán, who heads the ultranationalist Fidesz party, addressed the nation with a heated speech against refugees and Muslims. In the annual state of the nation speech, he claimed that refugees and migrants had descended on Hungary as part of a planned "Islamization" of Europe, saying that Hungary was the last defender of Christian Europe as "dark clouds are gathering" over the continent.[7] "We are those who think that Europe's last hope is Christianity.... If hundreds of millions of young people are allowed to move north, there will be enormous pressure on Europe. If all this continues, in the big cities of Europe there will be a Muslim majority," Orbán boldly proclaimed.

Orbán placed the blame, at least partially, on George Soros, the eighty-six-year-old Jewish Hungarian American billionaire, Holocaust survivor, and philanthropist, alleging that there was a conspiracy to create "the Soros-type of man" out of every European. While Soros shares a great deal of blame for the neoliberal economic policies his Open Society Foundations have pushed, there was no missing the anti-Semitism deeply ingrained in Orbán's ongoing campaign against him. The Orbán-led government had for years blamed Soros for the country's ills, drawing on age-old anti-Semitic conspiracy theories of a conniving Jew controlling the world from behind the scenes.

When I spoke to Hungarian journalist Bálint Bárdi in November 2017, he described the fever-pitch allegations against Soros as part of the government's efforts to "exploit the xenophobic feelings" of many Hungarians. "They say there is a threat to our country from the migrants, from the politicians in Brussels or George Soros ... and that the government is the only one that can defend Hungarian society."[8]

With xenophobia spiraling out of control, Orbán was well-placed to win the April elections and maintain his lordship over Hungary. Lydia Gall, a researcher at Human Rights Watch, described Orbán's attacks on Soros as cynical exploitation, drawing on "stereotypes that have been floating around against Jews for eons."[9]

Orbán's campaign against Soros and refugees helped his Fidesz party become the most extreme right-wing party in the country, successfully dislodging Jobbik, a far-right party with neo-Nazi roots. In December 2017, Cas Mudde, an expert on far-right politics and associate professor in the School of Public and International Affairs at the University of Georgia, explained that Fidesz was "effectively dominating 'their' [Jobbik] themes of authoritarianism, nativism and populism."[10]

On April 8, 2018, Orbán was reelected when his Fidesz party won by a landslide.[11] The prospects are bleak, and Hungary's anti-fascist movement is small and marginalized.

FRANCE

Meanwhile in France, the start of 2018 saw the far-right National Front attempt to reinvent itself as a mainstream populist party, a strategy that had seen success with the Alternative for Germany (AfD) and the FPO in Austria.

In the preceding two years, Marine Le Pen, the party's leader, rose and fell, losing to neoliberal banker Emmanuel Macron in the 2017 presidential elections. Nonetheless, Le Pen had won the backing of a majority of working-class voters in the first round of those elections, causing concern. It was part of an ongoing strategy, which had proven largely successful, of poaching voters from the low-income communities where the left had lost favor. The National Front has joined the legions of Eurosceptic parties calling for France's exit from the eurozone and the European Union and refocusing on disparaged European workers.

Despite its rebranding, the National Front could not escape its past, and many French leftists and anarchists vowed to keep that memory well preserved in the minds of the country's downtrodden. Founded in 1972 by Jean-Marie Le Pen, a Holocaust denier and virulent racist, the party has a lengthy history of alliances with far-right authoritarians, among them Russia's Vladimir Putin and Iraq's Saddam Hussein. Echoing the drivel of others like them, the National Front has alleged that France is one of the most damaged victims of "Islamization" in Europe.

With the newly inaugurated Macron in office, prospects for a better future were slim. Macron vowed to crack down on asylum seekers and the so-called radicalization of Muslim migrant communities. Anti-fascists were prepared.

Throughout the elections, anti-fascists mobilized across the country, fighting back against the surge in racism and Islamophobia. On April 23, 2017, just days after Le Pen had made it into the runoff against Macron, hundreds of anti-fascists squared off with police in Paris, pounding them with bottles, stones, and firecrackers.[12] Rejecting the false dichotomy between the far right and neoliberalism, they chanted: "No Marine, no Macron!"

ITALY

With far-right populism on the rise in Italy, parties such as CasaPound and Forza Nuova could openly describe themselves as fascists, Guido Caldiron, a Rome-based journalist and expert on the Italian far right, told me in January 2018.

While neither party had much hope for winning seats in the upcoming elections, which were slated for March 2018, the parties had a profound impact on the national discourse, stoking antimigrant xenophobia and promoting a worldview of ethnic and racial purity.

"This new wave goes along with the growth of the right in general in Italy. . . . They have been legitimized since the Berlusconi era of the nineties," Caldiron said. "The fact that they call themselves fascists is no longer a scandal."

Both parties had been engaged in violence against asylum

seekers and anti-fascists alike, and anti-fascists had responded by standing up against their bigotry and hate.

On February 19, anti-fascists rallied against CasaPound in Naples. Police officers wearing riot gear attacked them as they approached a hotel where CasaPound leader Simone Di Stefano was meeting with supporters. At least twenty people were arrested, and two required medical treatment, according to local media reports at the time.[13]

The crackdown on anti-fascists came just weeks after some twenty thousand people rallied in Macerata following a drive-by shooting that left six African migrants injured.[14] That attack was allegedly carried out by a former local candidate for the Northern League, a far-right populist party that subsequently pledged to deport hundreds of thousands of refugees and migrants to their home countries.

On March 5, 2018, Italians took to the ballot box for national elections. The vote saw large gains for far-right parties that formed an electoral coalition, including the League, the Brothers of Italy, and former prime minister Silvio Berlusconi's Forza Italia. Bound together by a collective Euroscepticism, the far-right parties were poised to strike a deal to form a government with the antiestablishment, populist Five Star Movement.[15]

CROATIA

In Croatia, the far right was at once distant from the corridors of power and close to the ruling elite's agenda. Shortly after the inauguration of U.S. president Donald Trump, a band of neo-Nazis from the pro-Ustaše Autochthonous Croatian Party of Right (A-HSP) rallied to support the billionaire-turned-leader in front of the U.S. embassy in Zagreb in February 2017.[16] Although the embassy and Croatia's mainstream political elite issued a slew of condemnations, the cozy relationship between the ideas of the radical right and the country's ruling Croatian Democratic Union (HDZ) party was clear.

With anti-fascist monuments and symbols under attack from the state and vigilantes alike, anti-fascists found themselves engaged primarily in a campaign to fight historical revisionism. With a largely successful demonization of socialism and anti-fascism underway, Lovro Krnić, editor of the *Anti-Fascist Courier*, told me that the "biggest problem" was building a sustainable anti-fascist movement when the bulk of otherwise fringe neofascist ideas were encapsulated in the government itself and often echoed by the country's liberals, ever fearful of being labeled "communists" by the right wing.

GERMANY

In September 2017, the Alternative for Germany (AfD) became the first far-right populist party to enter the German Bundestag since the Second World War, winning more than ninety seats. Founded as a Eurosceptic party just four and a half years earlier, the AfD had failed to gain the minimum 5 percent required to enter the Bundestag in 2013. Its rise was sudden and devastating for its political opponents, among them anti-fascists, refugees, and migrants.

The party, which denied claims of harboring fascist sympathies, made attacking asylum seekers and Muslims its bread and butter, gaining more than 5.8 million votes in the 2017 elections.

Former members cast doubt on the party's claim to reject racism and xenophobia. Bernd Lucke, the AfD's first leader, resigned in 2015 and accused the party of "Islamophobic and xenophobic" positions.[17]

The rise of Germany's far right was accompanied by a spike in extremist violence, with at least 3,533 documented attacks on refugees or refugee accommodations across the country in 2016.[18]

Anti-fascists prepared for the new challenge in which the AfD was no longer simply a party with politicians in regional governments but was now able to influence the country's policies from the Bundestag. On the night of the elections, thousands flooded the streets of Berlin and elsewhere to rally against the party's newfound success. "Nazis out," they shouted. "All of Berlin hates the AfD," others chanted.[19]

On February 17, 2018, when the AfD cynically attempted to host a "women's march," which focused on the party's alleged concern for the rights of women in Muslim-majority countries, around nine hundred anti-fascists gathered to block them from advancing.[20]

UNITED KINGDOM

On June 23, 2016, citizens of the United Kingdom took to the polls to vote on the country's future in the European Union. By the end of the tallying, 51.9 percent had voted to leave the bloc.[21] While many segments of the left had long articulated nuanced criticisms of the European Union and advocated their opposition to it, the Brexit campaign signified the mainstreaming of the British far right, with the campaign to leave channeling racist anger at immigrant workers and others. Since the 1990s, the United Kingdom Independence Party (UKIP), a far-right populist party, had pushed for the United Kingdom's departure from the alliance. In 2016, UKIP and its more mainstream allies found a voice among the general population, convincing a slim majority that leaving the bloc was the best option.

In the month following the referendum, hate crimes in England and Wales soared by 41 percent.[22] July 2016 saw 5,468 documented hate crimes, compared to 3,886 during the same month in 2015, the U.K.'s Home Office reported.

Throughout 2016, anti-Muslim hate crimes rose by a total of 47 percent in the U.K., according to hate monitor Tell MAMA.[23] Some 69 percent of the attackers were white men, while 59 percent of the victims were Muslim women. Migrant workers from Portugal, Poland, Romania, and elsewhere were also targeted in a spate of far-right violent incidents.

With xenophobia spiraling out of control, anti-fascists also took to the streets to oppose the hate being spewed by groups including the English Defense League (EDL) and Britain First. On April 1, 2017, hundreds of anti-fascists moved to shut down a rally held by the two groups in London, where far-right media figure Tommy Robinson had made an appearance.[24] "EDL, go to hell," they chanted. "Nazi scum off our streets," others yelled through megaphones. When confrontations erupted, police moved in and arrested twelve people during the first few hours of the rally and counterprotest.

On June 24, 2017, around fifty EDL demonstrators rallied in central London, while some 250 Britain First supporters gathered in Birmingham. In London, anti-fascists clashed with the EDL demonstrators, despite the far-rightists enjoying a police escort.[25]

While anti-fascist resistance was widespread, with activists working to ensure no far-right rally passed without being confronted, the threat of the far right remained severe. After Brexit, the Islamophobic and anti-immigrant rhetoric that had been fought by U.K. anti-fascists in the 1980s was stronger than ever.

GREECE

In Greece, the neofascist Golden Dawn party had been largely unable to build its ranks after the electoral successes it enjoyed in 2013 and 2015, despite the country being hit hard by the refugee crisis since 2015.

Golden Dawn was limited in its capacity for street violence, largely because, following the September 2013 murder of anti-fascist rapper Pavlos Fyssas, the group was on trial for allegedly operating a criminal organization. Though there had been years of brutal attacks on refugees, immigrants, and political opponents, that killing was the peak of neofascist violence on the streets of Greece.

In January and February 2018, Golden Dawn proved it was still a force to be reckoned with when it infiltrated mainstream nationalist protest movements, such as a pair of rallies against negotiations between Athens and Skopje over the use of the name "Macedonia."[26] Those rallies came just weeks after Keerfa, an Athens-based anti-fascist group, reported that more than thirty homes providing residence to Pakistani migrant laborers had been attacked in Piraeus, the port city near the capital.

Following the first rally on January 21, when hundreds of thousands came out in the streets of Thessaloniki, far-right assailants set an anarchist squat on fire in the northern coastal city. Later in the day, a Holocaust monument was vandalized and spray-painted with Golden Dawn logos.

On February 4, around 140,000 people repeated the "Macedonia is Greece" rally in the capital. Fearing yet more far-right attacks, anti-fascists—among them anarchists and leftists—organized to defend refugee squats throughout the city and to prevent attacks on Exarchia, an anarchist and anti-fascist stronghold in central Athens.

Nasim Lomani, an activist at the City Plaza squat, which provided residence to upward of 350 refugees and migrants, told me on the day of that rally: "All the squats are ready to protect themselves in case of any fascist attack. There are fascists coming from all over Greece, so we have to be careful."[27]

The night passed without the far right successfully carrying out any attacks. Despite the threat of a fascist resurgence, Greece's anti-fascist movement had shown its resilience. Yet, with growing anger at the self-described leftist party in power, Syriza, and widespread anxiety over the ongoing economic crisis, that threat was not going away any time soon.

THIS BOOK

These summaries are just a few examples of how the germs of populism, Islamophobia, antirefugee xenophobia, and racism were well nurtured across Europe going into 2018. The violence that stems from the far right's worldview was growing more visible—and more dangerous. Anti-fascists faced a plethora of challenges that also included the state and the police, which often harbored sympathies for fascists and neofascists and antipathy toward anti-fascists, leftists, and anarchists.

This book is not an academic undertaking and is not a conclusive study of anti-fascist movements and their tactics in challenging the far right. Neither is it a historical study of anti-fascism or the far right. By necessity, the book is largely limited to the five countries I visited while writing it. It is a journalistic endeavor, and, as such, much of its focus is on human stories. As suggested by its title, this book seeks only to provide snapshots of various anti-fascist movements, to open a window into the lives of anti-fascists who have risked their safety, careers, and much more to fight racism and fascism in every form. While many mainstream media outlets focus solely on direct confrontations, inflating the role of violence in anti-fascism, this book explores the myriad ways anti-fascists fight the far right and build a culture and society based on equity, equality, and justice.

Many of the anecdotes, interviews, and stories in this book first appeared in my reporting at *Al Jazeera English* between 2016 and 2018. That reporting is cited throughout the book and has been vastly expanded from its original form.

In the first chapter, I examine the role of anti-fascists in Germany. Through the story of Irmela Mensah-Schramm, a seventy-year-old pensioner who has painted over neo-Nazi graffiti and defaced far-right propaganda for more than three decades, I explore the rise of the far right, chiefly the Alternative for Germany. Mensah-Schramm's one-person anti-fascist struggle had resulted in a hand injury, legal problems, and a slew of threats, many of them against her life.

The second chapter delves into Greece, where a rich anti-fascist tradition continues to inform contemporary activism. Among the people profiled are the mother of an anti-fascist rapper who was killed by the Golden Dawn, the founder of an anti-fascist gym in Athens, and the activists who have occupied abandoned buildings to provide safe shelter to refugees and migrants facing the ever-present threat of far-right violence, arrest, and deportation.

Then, in chapter 3, we turn to Slovakia, where the story of the anti-fascist movement centers around Ján Benčík, a retired phone technician who made it his mission to track neofascists, to expose their activities by doxing them, posting their information online, and often to draw links between violent incidents and parliamentarian politicians from the Kotleba—People's Party Our Slovakia, a neo-Nazi outfit.

Chapter 4 focuses on several anti-fascists who led the fight against the far right in Italy, where neofascist groups such as CasaPound and Forza Nuova were on the rise. Adelmo Cervi, a seventy-four-year-old whose father and six uncles were murdered by fascists during the Second World War, is one of those activists. He has spearheaded efforts to educate young people about the dangers posed by the far right, seeking to inform them about the history of fascism in Italy. I also examine the struggles of young anti-fascist activists in Ostia, a suburb of Rome where Casa-Pound had made inroads in local elections in November 2017, and the position of refugees, migrants, and solidarity activists in the broader anti-fascist struggle.

The fifth chapter looks at Croatia, where the main forum of anti-fascist activity takes place in the historical discourse. With far-rightists and neofascists attempting to erase the country's crimes from the Second World War and to demonize the role of wartime anti-fascists and partisans, anti-fascists found themselves fighting against historical revisionism with the hope of changing the country's future. With neofascist themes overlapping those of the mainstream political right, the challenges were ample.

The final chapter follows the perilous trek of one Syrian refugee, Ramadan, to Germany only to encounter racism and the threat of violence. Examining Ramadan's story in the broader context of rising neofascism, far-right populism, and racist violence, the chapter explores the challenges anti-fascists face moving forward.

NOTES

1. Given the confines of this book's subject, it does not set out to examine the history of white nationalism, racism, fascism, neofascism, and white supremacy in North America.

2. Ishaan Tharoor, "Hungary's Leader Says He's Defending Christian Europe. The Pope Disagrees," *Washington Post*, April 10, 2018, https://www.washingtonpost.com/news/worldviews/wp/2018/04/10/the-popes-challenge-to-orban-and-europes-far-right/?utm_term=.77968338b8d5.

3. Patrick Strickland, "Refugees in Greece's Chios Fear Violence from Far-Right," *Al Jazeera English*, July 5, 2016, https://www.aljazeera.com/indepth/features/2016/06/refugees-greece-chios-fear-violence-160622125507719.html.

4. "Neo-fascists and Far-Right: Conquering Europe," *BlogActiv*, April 12, 2017, https://eulogos.blogactiv.eu/2017/12/04/neo-fascists-and-far-right-conquering-europe/.

5. Francois Murphy and John Revill, "Thousands Protest against Austrian Government's Shift to the Right," *Reuters*, January 13, 2018, https://www.reuters.com/article/us-austria-government-protests/thousands-protest-against-austrian-governments-shift-to-the-right-idUSKBN1F20PZ.

6. Jon Stone, "Austria's Far-Right Interior Minister Sparks Outrage after Saying Migrants Should Be 'Concentrated'," *Independent*, January 15, 2018,

https://www.independent.co.uk/news/world/europe/austria-far-right-fpo-migrants-concentrated-herbert-kickl-a8159541.html.

7. Daniel Boffey, "Orbán Claims Hungary Is Last Bastion against 'Islamisation' of Europe," *Guardian*, February 18, 2018, https://www.theguardian.com/world/2018/feb/18/orban-claims-hungary-is-last-bastion-against-islamisation-of-europe.

8. Patrick Strickland, "What's behind Hungary's Campaign against George Soros?," *Al Jazeera English*, November 22, 2017, https://www.aljazeera.com/news/2017/11/hungary-campaign-george-soros-171122120334509.html.

9. Ibid.

10. Patrick Strickland, "How Is Hungary's Far Right Changing?," *Al Jazeera English*, December 12, 2017, https://www.aljazeera.com/news/2017/12/hungary-changing-171209110936676.html.

11. "Viktor Orban: Hungary PM Re-elected for Third Term," *BBC*, April 9, 2018, http://www.bbc.com/news/world-europe-43693663.

12. "Protesters Clash with Paris Police Following French First-Round Result," *Deutsche Welle*, April 23, 2017, http://www.dw.com/en/protesters-clash-with-paris-police-following-french-first-round-result/a-38554227.

13. "Italian Far-Right Parties Met with Antifascist Protests in Venice, Naples, Bologna," *The Local*, February 19, 2018, https://www.thelocal.it/20180219/forza-nuova-casapound-antifascist-protests-bologna-naples-venice.

14. Lorenzo Tondo, "Attacks on Immigrants Highlight Rise of Fascist Groups in Italy," *Guardian*, February 6, 2018, https://www.theguardian.com/world/2018/feb/06/attacks-on-immigrants-highlight-rise-of-fascist-groups-in-italy.

15. Jon Henley, "Populists' Rise to Power in Italy Sets Perilous Precedent for EU," *Guardian,* May 17, 2018, https://www.theguardian.com/world/2018/may/17/populists-rise-to-power-in-italy-sets-perilous-precedent-for-eu.

16. Sven Milekić, "US Condemns Croatian Neo-Nazi March for Trump," *Balkan Insight*, February 27, 2017, http://www.balkaninsight.com/en/article/us-condemns-zagreb-neo-nazi-march-for-trump-02-27-2017.

17. Noah Barkin, "German AfD Founder Leaves Party Decrying Xenophobic Shift," *Reuters*, July 8, 2015, https://www.reuters.com/article/us-germany-politics-eurosceptics/german-afd-founder-leaves-party-decrying-xeno-phobic-shift-idUSKCN0PI25720150708.

18. Harriet Agerholm, "Germany Has Seen an Increase in Violence since It Opened Its Doors to Refugees . . . due to Attacks on Refugees," *Independent*, February 26, 2017, https://www.independent.co.uk/news/world/europe/ref-ugee-attacks-germany-ten-angela-merkel-hate-crime-a7600616.html.

19. "Thousands of AfD Opponents Demonstrate in Major Cities across Germany," *The Local*, September 25, 2017, https://www.thelocal.de/20170925/hundreds-of-afd-opponents-demonstrate-in-major-cities-across-germany.

20. "Protesters Scuffle with Police at AfD Demonstration," *Euronews*, February 18, 2018, http://www.euronews.com/2018/02/18/protesters-scuf-fle-with-police-at-afd-demonstration.

21. Alex Hunt and Brian Wheeler, "Brexit: All You Need to Know about the UK Leaving the EU," *BBC*, May 10, 2018, http://www.bbc.com/news/uk-pol itics-32810887.

22. Lizzie Dearden, "Hate-Crime Reports Rise by Almost a Third in Year as Home Office Figures Illustrate EU-Referendum Spike," *Independent*, October 17, 2017, https://www.independent.co.uk/news/uk/crime/hate-crimes-eu-ref erendum-spike-brexit-terror-attacks-police-home-office-europeans-xeno phobia-a8004716.html.

23. Aina Khan, "Tell MAMA: Most Islamophobic Attackers are White Men," *Al Jazeera English*, November 3, 2017, https://www.aljazeera.com/news/2017/11/mama-islamophobic-attackers-white-men-171103093605875.html.

24. Sarah Ann Harris, "EDL And Anti-Fascist Marches in London Cause Clashes," *HuffPost*, April 1, 2017, https://www.huffingtonpost.co.uk/entry/edl-britain-first-anti-fascist-marches-london_uk_58dfac2de4b0b3918c83 e5f1.

25. Samuel Osborne, "EDL and Anti-fascists Clash with Police in London," *Independent*, June 25, 2017, https://www.independent.co.uk/news/uk/home-

news/edl-english-defence-league-anti-fascists-clash-police-london-britain-first-birmingham-a7807401.html.

26. Patrick Strickland, "Tensions High in Athens ahead of Nationalist Rally," *Al Jazeera English*, February 4, 2018, https://www.aljazeera.com/news/2018/02/tensions-high-athens-nationalist-rally-180203221505840.html.

27. Ibid.

ALERTA!

ALERTA!

GERMANY

A grin stretched the width of Irmela Mensah-Schramm's face as she adjusted the brace on her gauze-swaddled right hand and lifted a binder full of photos detailing three decades of defacing neo-Nazi graffiti and propaganda in public spaces.[1]

It was March 2017, and seventy-year-old Mensah-Schramm told me she had painted over or defaced more than one hundred thousand manifestations of far-right graffiti and stickers throughout the previous thirty-one years. Her one-person anti-fascist battle left her with an injured hand for which she underwent surgery and landed her in a lengthy legal struggle against criminal charges related to vandalism. "I can't stand this," the retired teacher said of her hand injury, sitting in her second-story flat on the outskirts of Berlin. "It is a catastrophe for me."

Tossing her short gray bangs from in front of her spectacles with a quick head jerk, she flipped through the pages, boasting of painting over and reconfiguring neo-Nazi and antirefugee slogans on walls in cities, towns, and villages across Germany and, to a lesser extent, in neighboring countries such as the Czech Republic and Austria. In court in 2016, the judge prompted her to admit to the vandalism charges and to promise to stop defacing public property. "I just said I'd keep doing it," she recalled, letting out the kind of voracious chuckle normally expected from children. The court slapped her with a fine, but she vowed never to pay it.

Germany's far right includes populist parties, such as the Alternative for Germany (AfD), anti-Muslim groups, and neo-Nazi organizations. In recent years, other far-right groups have focused the bulk of their energy on antirefugee advocacy.

Sitting in her living room, Mensah-Schramm recalled the first time she defaced neo-Nazi graffiti back in 1986. Watching light posts speed by from her seat on the bus, she spotted a pro-Hitler sticker and quickly slapped the stop button above her. Within minutes, she had peeled away the sticker and left only unidentifiable adhesive in its place. She was scolded for arriving to work late that day, but she was never again able to leave far-right graffiti, stickers, or posters intact.

For the last three decades, threatening letters, voicemail messages with promises of violence, physical attacks, and police warnings to stop provoking far-rightists have failed to deter her.

"Ladies first," she giggled, pouring herself a steaming tea from a blackened kettle before filling the rest of the glasses placed on small oak coasters atop the coffee table. After she gulped down one tea and then another, she slipped on her sandals and prepared herself for the day before heading down to the bus stop across from her home.

On the bus, she sat with folded hands, a large smile ever-present on her face, as she headed for an anti-fascist counterprotest that challenged a far-right rally against the German government's migration policies. She opened her purse to make sure she brought her scraper for any stickers she might encounter and a small bottle of white-out correction fluid in case she needed to paint over any graffiti. When she doesn't have paint handy, she explained, she uses nail polish remover to erase the hate-filled messages.

She eventually exited at a railway station and boarded a train to the city center. Along the way, she punched in the password on her phone and flashed before-and-after images of her latest work. In the first photo, a far-right vandal had painted a gaggle of swastikas over an "Antifa" tag. In the second, Mensah-Schramm had transformed the black Nazi symbols into bright red hearts.

Although in the past she had encountered mostly anti-Semitic and neo-Nazi messages on the walls of buildings, on the sides of trains, and on lampposts, she said there had been a huge increase in Islamophobic and antirefugee graffiti since the rise of the several far-right groups and the beginning of the refugee crisis that gripped Europe in recent years.

The train ground to a nervous halt at Mensah-Schramm's stop, and she escaped through the sliding doors. Visibly excited, she spotted a group of far-right activists with shaved heads and arms saturated with white supremacist tattoos. She confronted them. "Nazis out!" she scowled repeatedly, raising her middle finger just a few inches from one of their faces to taunt the hefty man. They stood like statues in momentary shock as she went on her way.

Down the escalator and outside, she stopped for a moment to

survey the far-right demonstration—dubbed "Merkel Must Go," referring to German Chancellor Angela Merkel—and glided across the square to a group of Antifa counterprotesters.

"GERMANY FOR THE GERMANS"

Organizers stood on a stage and addressed the few hundred far-right demonstrators who had assembled in the square behind the train station. The crowd erupted in jubilant hoots and hollers as antirefugee and anti-Muslim declarations were bellowed through the loudspeakers situated on each end of the stage. "We are not the ones to blame, we are not the bad ones. It's her fault," a woman on stage shrieked, blaming Merkel. Whipped into a frenzy, her audience chanted at a fever pitch: "Deportations, deportations!"

A man dressed in a black suit and crimson necktie sported a mask of far-right U.S. president Donald Trump's face. The turquoise sky was punctuated with a host of fluttering banners, pro-Trump placards, and German and Russian flags, among others. The audience swelled. Shaved heads and raggedy beards poured in aside clean-cut, middle-aged men in football jerseys and women in Sunday dresses. "Islamists not welcome," read a large black flag depicting the silhouette of a lance-wielding man on horseback chasing a fleeing family. That image was meant to mock prorefugee solidarity posters and flags emblazoned with a refugee family's silhouette. "Stop Islam," another banner said, this one brandishing the logo of Pegida, a far-right, Islamophobic group that operates in several European countries. "Africa is big enough," declared one placard in the middle of the crowd. A gang of chanters in the audience wore hoodies that celebrated National Socialism.

At one point, a well-known local journalist with a colorful mohawk was spotted in the crowd. Far-right demonstrators cornered him and pressured him out of their space as they chanted *"Lugenpresse"* (German for "lying press"), a phrase with anti-Semitic undertones that was commonplace during Adolf Hitler's Third Reich.

Thomas Witte, thirty years old, traveled to the protest some 275 kilometers from his hometown of Niederdorf in the state of Saxony, often cited as a hotbed of neo-Nazism and far-right sentiment. "Merkel's policy has to go," Witte told me, holding up a banner likening the German chancellor to Adolf Hitler. "We need a culture of conversation in Germany."

Witte implausibly insisted that he wasn't a fascist—or even right-wing. "Everything that's against Merkel's opinion is automatically considered right-wing," he argued. "And the way she reacts and has pushed her style of policy in the past few months —even a real dictator would envy her."

Nonetheless, Witte was a member of Heimattreue Niederdorf, a far-right organization that campaigned against refugees and migrants in his town. Critics often described the group's members as racists and neo-Nazis.

Identitäre Bewegung, or the Identitarian movement, is an extraparliamentary political movement that calls for stricter immigration restrictions, chiefly from Muslim-majority countries. Robert Timm, the group's Berlin-based spokesperson, admitted when I met him in an eastern Berlin café a few days after the rally that the movement is associated with the AfD, but he stressed that the Identitarians operate independently. A towering, raw-boned twenty-five-year-old architecture student with brown-rimmed glasses, side-parted hair, and an unkempt beard, Timm had been active in the movement since April 2016. He conceded that members of the group have political roots in neo-Nazi movements but dismissed it as youthful folly and a lack of political education. Unconvincingly, he described the group as "a conservative movement" and insisted that the Identitarians were "not far right."

Timm said he was once a believer in multiculturalism and that he is not a proponent of a white ethno-state but argued that migration is upending Germany's social and cultural balance. "Even in a rich country—it doesn't matter how rich it is—[migration] still has an effect on the society," he said, cautiously sipping an espresso. "We are not blaming them [refugees] for coming here, but I think that we as Europeans, as Germans, still have the right to be against that."

In August 2017, Timm was one of around fifteen activists who scaled Berlin's Brandenburg Gate and hung two broad banners.[2] One of them displayed the group's name, and the other read: "Secure borders—secure future."

In May of that year, Identitarians attempted to storm the Justice Ministry offices in Berlin, calling for Justice Minister Heiko

Maas to step down over the country's migration policies.[3] The provocative action and others like it have landed the Identitarians in hot water with German authorities. By October, at least four hundred members of the group across the country were under surveillance by domestic intelligence.[4] "The fact that you are under surveillance does not make you a criminal," Timm retorted.

In March, Hans-Georg Maassen, head of the domestic intelligence agency Bundesverfassungsschutz, told a local newspaper that the Identitarian movement was going through a process of "increasing radicalization."[5]

"People come here, they migrate and ... their parents are pretty liberal ... but these people do it [to] themselves because they find themselves in a Western society where they maybe feel they don't really belong, and then they try to find their own identity by, for example, turning to radical Islam," Timm said, arguing that "enforced patriotism" for German citizens and mass deportations of refugees and migrations are the only solutions for the country's supposed ailments. "If you consider yourself a Turkish nationalist [in Germany], then it's maybe time to move to Turkey," he offered as an example.

Using the oft-employed stereotype that Muslims will seek to install Islamic law in Europe, he said: "I think we have every right to just make sure that we [white Germans] stay a majority here in Germany because not just the demographic but the democratic aspect."

At the adjacent table, a gray-haired German man tried to read the newspaper. Eavesdropping, he shook his head disappointedly without looking in Timm's direction, frustration painted on his wrinkle-worn face. Although the group experienced a surge in sympathy in January 2015, when more than twenty-five thousand people participated in an Identitarian-led march, its active membership was estimated to be around five hundred people.[6]

While Timm maintained that Germans are sympathetic to the Identitarians' message, he admits that he has landed in the crosshairs of Antifa activists on several occasions. He had been doxed, and activists published his address online, leading to attacks in the streets and anti-fascists showing up at his home. "Pretty much every . . . two to three weeks there are [instances] when either people [from the Identitarian movement or AfD] get beaten up, or their homes are being breached, or their cars are getting smashed," he claimed.

Anette Schultner, an AfD member, insisted neither she nor her party is Islamophobic. Nonetheless, she said she didn't want to "see Sharia law" in Germany. "The asylum law should not encourage people to move here," she opined. "Our position is that we should invest in countries neighboring countries with wars so there are more camps for refugees there."

She argued that refugees and migrants, even those who work hard to integrate, are "a danger to German identity."

In her Berlin office, Ulla Jelpke, a spokesperson for the Die Linke (The Left) party, argued that far-right movements and parties exploit the socioeconomic anxiety of Germany's working class to whip up xenophobic sentiment. "They don't see that the right way is that the rich should give to the poor; they look at people who are even weaker than them and blame them for whatever [the poor] don't have," she said. "This is the area where the right populists work," she added. "It's not just the right-wing to blame but also the conservative government like the CDU and their coalition partners. They are using this message as people from the middle of [the political spectrum]."

In December 2016, Chancellor Merkel called for a ban of the Islamic full-face veil, a rightward shift from the previous stance of her Christian Democrats (CDU).[7] The party was reportedly drawing up plans to impose the ban in courts, during police checks, and while driving automobiles. While Merkel's party was poised to win the upcoming elections, the AfD was polling at 7 percent of the national vote in early May. The center-left Social Democrats (SDP) and the Greens were each estimated to receive 7 percent. "First of all, we need to fight against the neo-Nazis, who are often close to the AfD. We have to demand that everyone is treated equally—poor people here and not only to call for integration of refugees—the enemies are upstairs. In the whole world, Germany as well, the rich people . . . have enough for everybody if there is fair distribution," said Jelpke.

Arguing that far-right people exploit the working class and poor masses without ever fighting on their behalf, she said: "This type of nationalism puts Germans first before everyone else. . . . This is pure racism."

"They manage to get a lot of people from the center with nationalism" by eschewing the openly racist rhetoric and anti-

Semitism of traditional neo-Nazis, she added. "Although they may not openly say it, they are hardcore German nationalists and make it a holy thing. They don't want to mix with foreigners, and integration is off the table for them."

HISTORY OF ANTI-FASCISM

People like Mensah-Schramm, who challenge the growth of Germany's contemporary far right, are just the latest manifestation in a lengthy history of German anti-fascism. That history is punctuated with ample examples of effective tactics that include both nonviolent strategies and direct confrontation.

In 1924, the Red Front Fighters' League, tied to the Communist Party of Germany, was one of the first organizations to fight Nazis in the streets. Its membership is estimated to have reached 130,000 within five years. After Adolf Hitler's regime consolidated power, when he became chancellor in January 1933, harsh state repression led to dwindling public resistance. With the Nazis in full control, many of the Red Front's leaders were arrested, jailed, banished to camps, and executed. Others fled and joined the fight against fascism in Spain and elsewhere.

Anarcho-syndicalists continued publishing pamphlets and newspapers, calling for strikes and protests against the Third Reich. In 1936, however, the Gestapo carried out raids across the country and crippled the movement. Despite the numerous attempts to assassinate Hitler before and during the Second World

War, the world would not see his demise until he took his own life in a bunker on April 30, 1945, as allied forces closed in.

Later down the line, anti-fascism reemerged as a grassroots movement under the Soviet satellite state of the German Democratic Republic (GDR) in the eastern part of the country. Although anti-fascism was a key component of the state's mythos from its inception, a neo-Nazi movement blossomed in the punk rock scene during the 1980s. With authorities taking a hands-off approach, Antifa circles materialized and took matters into their own hands. Church groups and collectives of concerned citizens also campaigned against the social phenomenon, reaching out to young people and trying to offer them an alternative.

According to the logic of East Germany's ideology, the imposition of communism had eradicated the conditions that allow fascism to sprout. Confined by this ideology, the GDR's authorities were hesitant to crack down on neo-Nazis because they feared that recognizing their existence would lead to their growth. In 1989, a group of punks draped in leather jackets and wearing jeans hijacked the annual Labor Day protest in Potsdam and raised banners and placards to protest the nascent neofascist surge.

The punk rock scene and political allegiances within the football community were microcosms illustrating the broader dichotomy between neo-Nazis and anti-fascists, but the division within this subterranean counterculture was particularly stark, often leading to violence. Neo-Nazi attacks on anti-fascists were particularly intense in 1987 and 1988, with both women and men targeted. Anti-Nazi leagues and anti-fascist organizations were established to spread propaganda and to disrupt neofascist meetings.

Eastern Germany still has a particularly high concentration of neo-Nazis. Rand C. Lewis, a historian and author of *The Neo-Nazis and German Reunification*, cited a specific instance of police emboldening the broader far right in the spring of 1990, when officers stormed a National Alternative (NA) area in East Berlin.[8] The raid inadvertently pushed the NA into the national media spotlight, providing it with effective propaganda for recruitment. With journalists desperate for interviews, the NA began charging between 100 and 200 euros per media meeting.

In 1989, the infamous Berlin Wall—which had separated West Germany and the GDR for decades—came down. That incident paved the way for the reunification of the country and the end of the Stalinist state that had been erected in the country's east following the Second World War. But what soon followed was an intense focus on the growth of ultranationalism and neo-Nazi political activity in that part of the country.

A scandal that gripped the national and international media for three nights in August 1992 shone light on that societal shift. Under the watchful eye of passive police officers, hundreds of neo-Nazis attacked a housing development for asylum seekers in Rostock, the largest city in the northern German state of Mecklenburg-Vorpommern. "Rostock cemented the reputation of post-Wall eastern Germany as a new haven for neo-Nazism, and that reputation stuck," journalist Ben Knight explained in 2010.[9]

At the height of the riot, hundreds of neo-Nazis attacked the building with stones and Molotov cocktails. It was only by sheer luck that no one died. Academics and state officials attempted in subsequent years to chalk up the indifference of the police to the weakened institutions that were enduring a period of transition after the GDR's collapse.

"FEELING UNWELCOME"

In 2016 alone, there were at least 3,533 documented attacks on refugees or refugee accommodations across Germany, the Funke Media Group reported.[10] Those attacks injured at least 560 people, including forty-three children, according to the Interior Ministry, and another 217 refugee groups and volunteers were targeted. More than 890,000 asylum seekers reached Germany in 2015, according to the government's statistics.

Throughout 2016, the Amadeu Antonio Foundation, an organization that tracks racially motivated violence and far-right extremism, documented more than twenty-three thousand instances of right-wing extremism—a sharp increase compared to the previous year. Expressing concern about the proliferation of groups such as the Identitarian movement, the foundation noted an increasing acceptance of violence among those on the far right.[11] The National Democratic Party of Germany (NPD), a far-right group with neo-Nazi leanings, boasted of some five thousand members, while several other far-right extremist organizations were also on the rise.

On March 19, 2016, an asylum seeker from Pakistan took the stage at a protest and appealed for solidarity in the face of growing antirefugee sentiment in the Marzhan-Hellersdorf borough in the eastern part of the German capital.[12] "We have seen the worst that humanity can offer: the air strikes, the drone strikes, the wars," he told the crowd as an activist translated his words to German every few minutes. A large banner fluttered against the windows of an old, communist-era apartment building across the street: "Together against Nazis and racists—here and everywhere."

In a nearby refugee shelter operated by the People's Solidarity activist organization, twenty-two-year-old Loay Alhamedi explained that he fled his hometown of Raqqa owing to violence at the hands of the Syrian government and death threats from the Islamic State of Iraq and the Levant (ISIL, also known as ISIS). Alhamedi, who also worked with refugees at the shelter, made his way through the halls, greeting Syrian and Afghan families in Arabic and English, respectively. He explained that he never imagined escaping the bloodletting in his country to encounter threats and violence in Germany. Alhamedi added that German camp employees have also been threatened by hardline antirefugee activists. "I see that it's not possible for me to go on living in this area," he told me. "I have seen a lot of situations here with my own eyes, like the Nazis accosting people [refugees]."

While waiting for the train one day, Alhamedi was confronted by a young man and woman who verbally assaulted him. "That morning I heard my uncle was killed by the YPG, so I was already crying," he said, referring to the People's Protection Units, a Kurdish armed group in Syria. "They came to me threatening me, yelling in my face," he recalled. "They told me I came here to steal their money. I started yelling, I was crying. I told him, 'I didn't come here for money. . . . I spent six thousand euros [US$6,830] to get here.'"

Alhamedi noticed that right-wing demonstrations in the neighborhood had increased in recent months. "As far as I'm concerned, I don't care. They are free to express their opinions. But it has happened more than once that incidents like twelve or so young men gather usually late at night. . . . They hit [foreigners] with lead pipes."

Alhamedi wished he could speak to these attackers who target refugees. "I don't know if it's possible . . . but I wish I could make them understand . . . why Syrians are coming." He said that Syrians were not fleeing their homeland by choice but had to flee in order to survive. "What's the difference between a Syrian and a German anyway? In the end, we are both humans."

Back at the protest, flags from various progressive parties and movements beat against the cloudy afternoon sky. The Association of Anti-Fascists and Victims of the Nazi Regime, the

Left Party, the Greens, the Social Democratic Party of Germany, the Pirate Party—all were represented. Demonstrators held up placards in the crowd: "Berlin against Nazis," one read. "Nazis out!" another proclaimed.

After addressing the crowd, Petra Pau, vice president of the German Federal Parliament and senior member of the Left Party, came down from the stage. "The success of the AfD is not just about right now—it is the effect of a long process in German society," she said, arguing that Germans need to unite "365 days a year to fight racism."

Pau warned that the failure to prosecute those who attack refugee shelters will create an environment of impunity and lead to more violence. Raiko Hannemann, one of the demonstration organizers, echoed Pau. "It is also very important that [the protest] is happening here in this district because it has a very bad reputation," he told me. "Because in [recent] years there were a few incidents, attacks. . . . For us, it's very important to show that not only Nazis are living here."

Although the AfD had publicly condemned attacks on centers for asylum seekers, the party's rhetoric had fostered the anti-refugee sentiment that has gradually but steadily risen throughout the last year. Originally founded in 2013 as a Eurosceptic party, the AfD took the lead as the most aggressive antirefugee voice in the country while more than a million asylum seekers have arrived in Germany from 2015 to the present.

When I met him in March 2016, Georg Pazderski, the AfD's Berlin chairman, folded his arms on a large wooden table in a conference room at the party's local office and, from time to time, adjusted his watch under the cuff of his jacket sleeve. The party official, with hair slicked back, framed his opposition to refugees in religious and cultural terms, evoking stereotypes of them as illiterate and uneducated. "Imagine at what level we have to start with these people," he said, arguing that it is "almost impossible" for asylum seekers to integrate into German society. "I don't think that there is much ... possibility to integrate them in a way that they could stay in Germany. There is certainly a certain percentage that will manage it, but I think 90 percent will not manage it," he said with a gentle nod of confidence. "They're coming from a different culture, mainly with an Islamic background, mainly from different countries," Pazderski continued. "And they're coming to a Christian culture—and this is totally different."

With a dose of twisted logic, Pazderski blamed German chancellor Merkel's supposed open-door asylum policy for the violence. "There are some people who might [use] this antimigrant or antirefugee rhetoric," he said. "But on the other hand, who is responsible ... that something like this can happen?"

Pazderski denounced those who attack refugees as "misguided" but said a portion of the responsibility lies with the government. "We don't have to demonstrate in front of a refugee camp or something like that," he said. "We have to demonstrate in front of the office of the chancellor and of the parties."

Despite his claims that the AfD opposes violence, party members had already called for a crackdown on Muslims, and senior members had evoked violent rhetoric. In late March, a local branch of the AfD in lower Bavaria called for all mosques to be shut down by the government, according to local media. "Islam does not belong to Germany," the group wrote in a forty-five-page draft of party principles, suggesting a ban on the "construction and operation of mosques."

Some analysts argued that AfD members have incited people to violence, such as when the party's then leader, Frauke Petry, proclaimed that officers "should use firearms if necessary" in order to "prevent illegal border crossings."

Back at the refugee solidarity protest in Marzhan-Hellersdorf, organizer Raiko Hannemann said he hoped the AfD's success in the recent regional elections would serve as a "wake-up call" for Germans. "When I see this, I am already quite optimistic," he said, gesturing toward the crowd. A band on stage started up, a solidarity song echoing throughout the square. "But you don't see them in the news. What you see in the news is [some] Nazi attacks refugees, or [when] a Nazi attacks a political opponent."

VIOLENCE CONTINUED

During the first half of 2017, attacks on refugees and migrants were still prevalent, and such incidents showed signs of having been carefully planned and executed. The Amadeu Antonio Foundation warned of further radicalization among far-right extremists. In places like Dresden, where neo-Nazi movements have a stronger presence, attacks were more frequent than in liberal enclaves like Berlin. Nonetheless, such acts of violence also occurred in urban centers across the country.

On July 9, in Saxony, the foundation recorded an attack by two far-right drunkards targeting a Libyan asylum seeker. Strolling the streets after 2:00 AM, the pair of men assaulted and injured the man with a glass bottle. "Heil Hitler," they shouted as they carried out the attack.

Just a week earlier in the Bavaria region, a pair of young men kicked a twenty-four-year-old Syrian refugee until he lost consciousness. The victim's nose was fractured and his face covered in bruises. A day earlier in Saarland, assailants set ablaze a building that was being converted into refugee housing. These attacks and others like them were commonplace throughout 2016 and 2017. As was the case in several other countries, far-right radicalization found a home online, with social media networks becoming full of antirefugee and Islamophobic incitement. The online racism took a variety of forms, according to another report by the Amadeu Antonio Foundation.[13]

The proliferation of false news about refugees and Muslims was accompanied by an uptick in posts expressing cultural racism, nationalism, and dehumanization of refugees that fostered distrust in media portrayals of refugees and tarnished volunteers and workers affiliated with refugees as "left-wing extremists." The abuse was often coupled with anti-Semitism and extreme sexism. The report also documented more than three hundred "No Homes" pages on Facebook—rejecting refugee accommodation. Most of them expressed hatred of refugees, arguing that they would ruin the local culture and that refugees were incapable of successfully integrating into society. Others were explicitly violent. The foundation cited additional research that found more than a quarter of Germans sympathized with right-wing views, while another 44 percent viewed antirefugee agitation favorably. "Organized right-wing extremists mostly mean their threats very seriously," the report explained, urging readers: "It is accordingly imperative to protect your own data, and to network and get organized with other people."

It went on to warn: "When you post statements in the social networks opposing Nazis or in favor of refugees, it is very probable that you will be attacked." The report concluded by stressing the imperative for refugee solidarity activists and anti-fascists to be prepared for self-defense by networking, seeking out allies, and exposing racist hate speech and those who espouse it.

ANTI-FASCISTS AND THE FAR RIGHT: TIT-FOR-TAT ATTACKS

During this period, Germany's far right did not limit its attacks to refugees and migrants, and often targeted anti-fascists and others who mobilized against its political vision. In January 2016, just days after reports of mass sexual assault by refugees in Cologne captured international headlines, more than a thousand members of the anti-Muslim Pegida group rallied in the city, calling for Germany to seal its borders to refugees and migrants fleeing war and economic devastation.[14] "Refugees not welcome," their banners proclaimed. Heavily armed police separated the group from anti-fascist counterprotesters who gathered a few hundred yards away. Although the Pegida activists and their cohorts accused refugees of being behind the sexual assault, it later emerged that the number of asylum seekers involved in the violence had been vastly exaggerated by far-right groups. The far-right activists hurled glass bottles at police officers and erected barricades, but only four people were arrested by that afternoon.

In June 2016, Germany's domestic intelligence body warned that xenophobic and antirefugee violence was spiraling out of control. Explaining that 114 attacks targeted refugee accommodations in the first five months of the year, the agency said that 66 percent of them were carried out by assailants who were previously unknown as affiliates or members of the far-right scene.[15]

On September 4, 2016, a group of anti-fascists clashed with AfD supporters who had gathered at a pub in Munich to celebrate electoral gains after the party ranked second in the Mecklenburg–Western Pomerania elections. The party gained 21 percent of the vote and beat out Merkel's ruling CDU party.

Far-right rapper Chris Ares, writing on Facebook after the incident, accused some thirty anti-fascists of starting the violence after arriving with batons and pepper spray. "You know where to find us. You can come with 100 people against three of us, we are men of honor, we stand or we die," he wrote in the post.

Witnesses provided a much different account, arguing that

Ares and AfD members charged the protesters and sparked the fighting. One witness alleged that Ares was "running madly into the crowd attacking everything in front of him."

A journalist who was present said the anti-fascists weren't armed, and photos that later emerged supported the reporter's account. A Facebook account linked to Antifa groups said the AfD supporters "brutally attacked demonstrators and journalists with punches and kicks," while others recalled the far-rightists hurling homophobic invective at the anti-fascists as they assaulted them.

While much ink has been spilled examining the exact ideological nature of the AfD—debating whether it is indeed a neo-Nazi group—party member Björn Höcke spelled it out in January 2017.[16] Railing against what he viewed as an unnecessary legacy of national guilt for the Holocaust, Höcke employed a not-so-subtle term that was in wide currency during the Third Reich's reign. "The AfD is the last revolutionary, the last peaceful chance for our fatherland," he told supporters in a beer hall. When he argued that "German history is handled as rotten and made to look ridiculous," the crowd replied with ultranationalist fervor by chanting: "Deutschland! Deutschland!"

"Beloved friends, we must do little less than make history, so that there will be for us Germans, us Europeans, a future," he said, prompting applause and cheers from the audience. "We can make history, and we are doing it."

Indeed, the AfD was making history—and it was successfully redefining the publicly acceptable parameters of German political discourse. But it wasn't doing so without opposition. Organizers of that event did not make public the precise location of the meeting until the day it took place, fearing backlash and confrontation from anti-fascists.

On January 21, 2017, a day after far-right U.S. president Donald Trump was inaugurated in Washington, D.C., far-right parties from across Europe assembled in Koblentz to discuss their designs for Europe.[17]

"We are seeing the end of one world and the birth of a new," the leader of France's National Front, Marine Le Pen, said inside the conference. Le Pen blasted Merkel for her refugee policies, arguing: "But no one asked the Germans what they think of this immigration policy."

Echoing Le Pen's criticism of Merkel, Matteo Salvini, leader of the far-right Northern League in Italy, claimed: "There are thousands of Italians without homes, electricity, or heating, while thousands of immigrants are living in hotels."

Outside, more than three thousand anti-fascists rallied against the conference. Speaking to the Associated Press news agency, Avaaz activist Pascal Vollenweider said anti-fascists hoped to deliver a "strong message" to the ultranationalist politicians because "global citizens are rejecting their old dangerous ideas."

Far-right attacks went beyond direct confrontations and firebombing refugee shelters. In October 2016, police across the country launched an investigation into revelations that at least fifteen of their officers had ties to the Reichsbürger, a far-right regional separatist group.[18] The Reichsbürger movement considers the country's 1937 borders, which had been vastly expanded under the Third Reich's war-hungry occupation regime, the legitimate parameters of Germany and claims that present-day Germany remains occupied by the Second World War's Allied Forces.

The much-feared problem was not limited to the police, either. In May 2017, a German military officer with far-right views planned an attack and tried to frame a Syrian refugee.[19] Named "Franco A" in the German media, the officer was arrested before he could successfully carry out the attack. "Prosecutors say that Franco A had extreme right-wing views and, along with a 24-year-old student who was arrested the same day, was plotting a terror attack with the apparent intention of framing it on a Syrian refugee," *Vice News* reported at the time.[20] The news sparked a sharp debate within Germany's armed forces and intelligence community when it came to light that the officer's far-right views had been known to the upper echelon for years. The scandal took place just weeks after the country's Federal Ministry of Defense revealed that 275 suspected right-wing extremists in the armed forces' ranks were being investigated. "We have to ask, systematically, how someone with such clear right-wing extremist views, who writes a master's paper with clearly nationalistic ideas . . . was able to continue to pursue a career in the Bundeswehr [armed forces]," Defense Minister Ursula von der Leyen told the press, ostensibly unaware of the obvious relationship between ultranationalism and militarism.

Coming less than a month after far-right claims to a bombing targeting the Dortmund Borussia soccer team, the proliferation of antirefugee and ultranationalistic ideas among the security forces did not bode well for the country's immediate future.[21]

RISE OF RACIST CONCERTS

In July 2017, right-wing radicals gathered at a neo-Nazi concert in Germany's Thuringia state and chanted "Sieg Heil"—the mantra used to salute Hitler during the Third Reich. The concert—dubbed "Rock against Being Swamped by Foreigners"—brought out an audience of more than six thousand people from across Europe. Left-wing politicians blasted local authorities for letting the event go on. "I find it intolerable that they staged a giant right-wing extremist rock festival under the guise of a demonstration and earned money for their political network while all the costs were passed on to taxpayers," Bodo Ramelow, Thuringia state premier and member of Die Linke, said in an interview with local press.[22] "I think we have to define the right to assembly precisely enough that in future local authorities, licensing offices and courts don't see things like this in terms of freedom of speech and treat a gigantic concert as a nice neighborhood demonstration," Ramelow said.

But warning signs had been present for years. "For us, music is an ideal medium for addressing young people," Frank Franz, a spokesperson for the NDP, told *Deutsche Welle* back in 2013.[23] "With this music, we can expand our circle of influence and, by doing so, establish nationalist content in all youth cultures," the NPD-linked group Nationale Sozialisten Rostock said.

Indeed, far-right concerts had been used as a tactic to expand political influence, particularly among the German youth in conservative areas. "There is a risk that Thuringia will become a haven for all types of extremists, since they must feel less exposed to persecution here," Thuringia state parliament member Andreas Bühl told a newspaper.

Throughout the first half of 2016, neo-Nazi concerts spiked in frequency and attendance, according to local media reports drawing on statistics from the Interior Ministry. More than ninety-eight neo-Nazi concerts were held during the first six months of that year. In the same period in 2015, a total of sixty-three neo-Nazi music events were held. The largest concert in 2016 drew an audience of around 3,500 people, while the largest of its kind a year earlier brought only 650 attendees. By the end of 2016, Germany saw 205 right-wing extremist concerts.

Well into 2017, attendance had yet to subside. In July, a concert attended by six thousand was held in the small town of Themar, home to a mere three thousand residents.[24] Outside the show, police stood between some two thousand anti-fascist protesters and the attendees, many of whom wore Nazi insignia and brandished symbols—forbidden by German law—of far-right extremist groups.

"NO ONE HAS THE RIGHT TO SPREAD NAZI PROPAGANDA"

Back at the protest in March 2017, the Antifa counterdemonstration grew larger than the far-right protest. In the middle of the crowd was a large inflatable bear—"Nazis out of Berlin" printed across its chest—swaying lightly with the wind. A vast banner held by the front line of anti-fascist protesters read: "No one has the right to spread Nazi propaganda." Another placard hung from a wall behind the Antifa gathering: "No one is illegal," it stated plainly.

Mensah-Schramm stood in the first row, her face gleaming and a middle finger raised in the direction of the far-right demonstrators. A group of far-right protesters sauntered over, a column of police separating the opposing sides. The tension was palpable amid a back-and-forth of obscenities and insults. Curse words hung in the air. The two protests thinned and eventually ended as the dimming sun gave way to dark night. Mensah-Schramm stuck around, searching the area for neo-Nazi stickers. Spotting a Pegida sticker on a nearby bus stop, she quickly pulled out her scraper and scratched it off. She moved through the lit alleyways and streets in the surrounding neighborhood. She checked lampposts and walls along the way. Eventually, she spotted "refugees out" scribbled in marker over a preexisting painting of a heart on a concrete ledge. She doused it in nail polish remover and scrubbed it into oblivion, leaving behind only the bright red heart in its place. "Voila," she exclaimed, bursting into brief storm of laughter.

Later, she recalled an incident in 2005 when death threats against her started appearing on the walls of homes and shops in her neighborhood. "Schramm, we will get you," the graffiti read. One of the young men responsible for the minatory graffiti eventually approached her and told her he had changed his views. "One exceptional day, he came up to me and said he wasn't a part of it anymore," she recounted. "We talked for a little bit, and he said he had been rethinking his choices because they were threatening and intimidating me so much, but I never gave up. We shook hands and I offered him help. That was a colossal experience for me."

Most on the far right, however, weren't so easily convinced by dialogue. For them, other means remained necessary. Six months later, the AfD gained more than ninety seats in parliamentary elections, landing it in the Bundestag for the first time. The challenges were only growing.

NOTES

1. Patrick Strickland, "Germany: 70-Year-Old Anti-fascist Defaces Neo-Nazi Art," *Al Jazeera English*, July 28, 2017, http://www.aljazeera.com/in depth/features/2017/06/germany-70-year-anti-fascist-defaces-neo-nazi-art-170622085119127.html.

2. Kate Brady, "Right-Wing Activists Scale Berlin's Brandenburg Gate," *Deutsche Welle*, August 27, 2016, http://www.dw.com/en/right-wing-activ-ists-scale-berlins-brandenburg-gate/a-19508752.

3. Alistair Walsh, "Far-Right Identitarian Movement Group Attempts to Storm German Justice Ministry," *Deutsche Welle*, May 19, 2017, http://www.dw.com/en/far-right-identitarian-movement-group-attempts-to-storm-german-justice-ministry/a-38904709.

4. Dick Wolfgang, "From Anti-Antifa to Reichsbürger: Germany's Far-Right Movements," *Deustche Welle*, October 22, 2016, http://www.dw.com/en/from-anti-antifa-to-reichsb%C3%BCrger-germanys-far-right-movements/a-36122279.

5. Ben Knight, "German Right-Wing Identitarians 'Becoming Radicalized,'" *Deutsche Welle*, March 20, 2017, http://www.dw.com/en/german-right-wing-identitarians-becoming-radicalized/a-38032122.

6. Ibid.

7. "Angela Merkel: Full-Face Veil Must Be Banned in Germany," *Al Jazeera English*, December 7, 2016, http://www.aljazeera.com/news/2016/12/angela-merkel-full-face-veil-banned-germany-161206130507492.html.

8. Rand Lewis, *The Neo-Nazis and German Reunification* (Westport, CT: Praeger, 1996), 27.

9. Ben Knight, "The Rise of the Far-Right in the East," *Deutsche Welle*, September 21, 2010, http://www.dw.com/en/the-rise-of-the-far-right-in-the-east/a-5996369.

10. "More than 3,500 Attacks on Refugees in Germany in 2016: Report," *Deutsche Welle*, February 26, 2017, http://www.dw.com/en/more-than-3500-attacks-on-refugees-in-germany-in-2016-report/a-37719365.

11. Alina Darmstadt and Stefan Lauer, "Verfassungsschutzbericht 2016: Mehr Nazis, mehr Gewalt, mehr Terror," *Belltower News*, July 4, 2017, http://www.belltower.news/artikel/verfassungsschutzbericht-2016-mehr-nazis-mehr-gewalt-mehr-terror-12245.

12. Patrick Strickland, "The Rise of Germany's Anti-refugee Right," *Al Jazeera English*, April 7, 2016, http://www.aljazeera.com/indepth/features/2016/03/rise-germany-anti-refugee-160331123616349.html.

13. Christina Dinar, Theresa Mair, Simone Rafael, Jan Rathje, and Julia

Schramm, "Hate Speech against Refugees in Social Media," Amadeu Antonio Foundation, 2016, http://www.amadeu-antonio-stiftung.de/w/files/pdfs/eng _hetze-gegen-fluechtlinge.pdf.

14. Lizzie Dearden, "Cologne Attacks: Police Use Water Cannon and Pepper Spray on Anti-immigration Pegida Protesters," *Independent*, January 9, 2016, http://www.independent.co.uk/news/world/europe/cologne-attacks -police-use-water-cannon-and-pepper-spray-on-anti-immigration-pegida- protesters-a6803996.html.

15. Ben Knight, "German Intel: More 'Turbo-Radicalized' Neo-Nazis Emerging," *Deutsche Welle*, July 5, 2016, http://www.dw.com/en/german- intel-more-turbo-radicalized-neo-nazis-emerging/a-19379532.

16. Max Fisher and Amanda Taub, "Germany's Extreme Right Challenges Guilt over Nazi Past," *New York Times*, January 18, 2017, https://www.ny times.com/2017/01/18/world/europe/germany-afd-alternative-bjorn-hocke .html.

17. "Thousands Protest over Far-Right Conference in Koblenz," *Al Jazeera English*, January 21, 2017, http://www.aljazeera.com/news/2017/01/thou sands-protest-conference-germany-170121135526441.html.

18. Marc Saha, "A Broken Oath: Reichsbürger in the Police Force," *Deutsche Welle*, October 31, 2016, http://www.dw.com/en/a-broken-oath- reichsb%C3%BCrger-in-the-police-force/a-36217758.

19. Tim Hume, "One German Soldier's Fake Syrian Refugee Terror Plot Stokes Fears of Hidden Military Extremism," *Vice*, May 5, 2017, https://news .vice.com/story/one-german-soldiers-fake-syrian-refugee-terror-plot-stok es-fears-of-hidden-military-extremism.

20. Ibid.

21. Justin Huggler, "German Police Investigate Far-Right link to Dortmund Bombing," *Telegraph*, April 16, 2017, http://www.telegraph.co.uk/news/2017/ 04/16/german-police-investigate-far-right-link-dortmund-bombing/.

22. Jefferson Chase, "Neo-Nazi Concert Raises Free Speech Concern," *Deutsche Welle*, July 17, 2017, http://www.dw.com/en/neo-nazi-concert-rais es-free-speech-concern/a-39722439.

23. Stefan Rheinbay, "Ensnaring Young People with Right-Wing Music," *Deutsche Welle*, April 26, 2013, http://www.dw.com/en/ensnaring-young-people-with-right-wing-music/a-16774494.

24. "Neo-Nazis Rock Small Town in Germany," *Deutsche Welle*, July 15, 2017, http://www.dw.com/en/neo-nazis-rock-small-town-in-germany/a-397 06498.

2

GREECE

On the breezy morning of March 31, 2017, a group of seven black-masked anarchists approached the headquarters of the neo-fascist Golden Dawn party near the Greek capital's Larissa Station, a central train stop in the densely populated working-class borough of Kolonos. Armed with sledgehammers, sticks, and road flares, many of them donned motorcycle helmets in anticipation of a fight with the far-right Golden Dawn members. But on this morning, they met no resistance. The anti-fascists quickly smashed the windows and threw flares into the office. Messages lambasting the Golden Dawn were spray-painted on the door. According to some accounts, those inside the office, unprepared for a confrontation, quickly fled. Security camera footage of the incident emerged in the local media within hours and went viral on social media.

In the video, taxis and other vehicles can be seen speeding past as a group of anarchists stayed back on the road to ensure they weren't ambushed from behind. Within minutes, the group had smashed the windows of the office, battered the door, and left behind glass shards glimmering under the bright spring sky. Emanating from large holes, weblike cracks stretched across the window panes.

The anti-fascists quickly disappeared from the camera's view and ostensibly retreated to Exarchia, a neighborhood known as a safe haven for anarchists and leftists who make it a point to prevent incursions by police and far-rightists alike.

Later that afternoon, police detained eleven individuals in relation to the attack. Within hours, however, they were set free. But a university student, Alexis Lazaras, who happened to walk by the office and snapped a quick video with his phone was not so lucky. Golden Dawn members tracked him down and beat him ruthlessly, leaving him bloody and bruised. He was later hospitalized. Local media reports suggested that the victim had nothing to do with the attack and was targeted, in the words of his assailants, for having the appearance of an anarchist.

That same day, Nikolaos Michaloliakos, the founder and leader of Golden Dawn, described the assault on his party's headquarters as left-wing "terrorism." He also denounced the attack on the university student, but police later arrested a forty-two-year-old party member—and former employee of Michaloliakos—for the attack. Attempting to save face, the far-right leader later fired the assailant.

On Saturday, April 3, less than a week later, thousands of antifascists amassed in Kolonos and made their way toward the Golden Dawn's headquarters. Making their way along the street, they chanted against the Golden Dawn and other neo-Nazi organizations. "Not in parliament, not anywhere. Smash fascism everywhere," the anarchists, communists, and antiracists sang in unison. They blocked traffic and marched through the city's corridors, eventually meeting a row of heavily armed police in riot gear. "Pavlos Fyssas lives. Smash the Nazis," they hollered, referring to an anti-fascist rapper who was stabbed to death in 2013 by an employee of Golden Dawn.

Standing in the front and shouting through a megaphone was Petros Constantinou, a frosty-haired city councillor and the national director of the antiracist group Keerfa. Constantinou later told me that the Golden Dawn built its base by attacking immigrants, leftists, trade unionists, and critics. They built small pockets of support in neighborhoods where police tolerated their presence.[1] "But we've always been an absolute majority against them," he explained. "The Golden Dawn tried to [expand] in some neighborhoods and in the islands. . . . In all of these campaigns, they've been defeated through thousands of demonstrations, one by one."

These tit-for-tat attacks and confrontations between anti-fascists and the Golden Dawn have punctuated the last few years of political turmoil in Greece, with the former accusing the police of playing an integral role of protecting the latter. And like any prolonged conflict, these battles have produced ample martyrs, idols, and intensely hated enemies for both sides.

THE RISE OF THE GOLDEN DAWN

In 1980, Michaloliakos established a national socialist journal called *The People's League of Golden Dawn*, which eventually grew into an organization of the same name, and in 1993 it was recognized as an official political party in Greece. Michaloliakos, who had spent time in prison in the 1970s after being discharged from the military for his involvement in political violence, viewed himself as the bearer of the brutal Greek military junta's legacy. Lasting from 1967 to 1974, that regime was characterized by political repression, torture, and the incarceration of dissidents.

A short, stocky man, Michaloliakos styled the party's political program on the ultranationalistic ideas of a greater Greece that encompassed territories in southern Albania, present-day Macedonia, and southern Bulgaria. For the Golden Dawn, politics were about the redemption of a Greece that had long since ceased to exist, from the conquest of Constantinople (present-day Istanbul) to the swallowing of Cyprus, the Mediterranean island that is home to both ethnic Greeks and Turks. Integral to these goals was the expulsion of ethnic and religious minorities, with Muslims playing a prominent role in the party's catalog of perceived enemies.

Throughout the 1990s, the Golden Dawn's objectives were hyperfocused on issues of identity in the Balkan region. The party hadn't seen much mainstream attention until the 1991–1992 naming dispute with the newly established Republic of Macedonia, formerly a unit of the Socialist Federal Republic of Yugoslavia. Greek nationalists, the Golden Dawn included, had seized on the dispute and claimed that the name "Macedonia" solely referred to the present-day region of northern Greece.

In the years that followed, many Golden Dawn members traveled to Yugoslavia to fight in the Greek Volunteer Guard alongside Serb forces operating under the leadership of President Slobodan Milošević. Many of those volunteer militiamen were later alleged to have been present during the Srebrenica massacre, the 1995 genocide of Muslim Bosniaks at the hands of Milošević-backed Serb fighters.

In the 1994 and 1996 parliamentary elections, the Golden Dawn participated and garnered around 0.1 percent and 0.07 percent of the vote, respectively. However, the poor parliamentary showing belied the growing street-level sympathy for the party's xenophobic, homophobic, and racist message. By the late 1990s and early 2000s, clashes between party members and anti-fascists were a regular feature of Greek life. While attempting to build a formidable street presence among working-class Greeks, the party also campaigned among high-school-aged youth and university students, targeting subcultures such as the punk scene. Throughout that period, the Golden Dawn sought like-minded allies across Europe, building lasting partnerships with the likes of the neo-Nazi National Democratic Party of Germany and the far-right Italian Forza Nuova (New Force).

In the mid-2000s, the party's ire was fixated on immigrants, particularly those who came from Muslim-majority countries. By 2010, onlookers and critics couldn't ignore the party's growth. In Athens that year, more than 5 percent of voters cast their ballot for Golden Dawn in municipal elections.

Campaigning on ideas such as planting land mines along the country's Turkish border and organizing so-called crime patrols in immigrant-heavy neighborhoods, the Golden Dawn secured nearly 7 percent of the national vote in 2012. And in June 2014, the group for the first time entered the European Parliament when it gained 9 percent of the vote, obtaining three chairs.

In 2015, with Greece suffocating under the weight of European debts, the Golden Dawn gained the third largest share of the votes—or seventeen parliamentary seats—in the same elections that brought to power the left-wing Syriza party. The contradictions of Greece's political landscape were stark.

HISTORY OF VIOLENCE

The Golden Dawn's calls for violence have often been enacted, and the group boasts a long history of targeting its political opponents, members of the LGBTQI community, immigrants, and refugees.

In October 2012, the United Nations refugee agency (UNHCR) said that eighty-seven racist attacks had been recorded between January and September of that year.[2] Often equipped with clubs, crowbars, and attack dogs, the attackers targeted undocumented migrants and refugees from places including Afghanistan, Bangladesh, Pakistan, and Somalia, among others. In many of the documented cases, the assailants were reportedly wearing Golden Dawn insignia.

But while the Golden Dawn can point to a nearly four-decade history, Greece's anti-fascist movement can boast of nearly double that. For anti-fascists, anarchists, and others on the far left, direct confrontation, including violent attacks, target not just

Golden Dawn and its far-right allies but also state institutions—namely, the police. A 2013 Reuters report, citing police data, said 527 arson and bomb attacks were carried out by anarchists and other leftist groups in 2012 alone, compared to the 542 recorded attacks in the twelve years following the 1974 collapse of the Greek military junta.

To a lesser extent, media outlets have been targeted for giving a platform to far-rightists, as in the case of an action carried out by Greek anarchists who raided a television station as a news presenter interviewed a Golden Dawn member in April 2012.[3] In mid-sentence, the presenter looked up beyond the camera. Within moments, he and his guest were covered in Greek yogurt thrown at them by anarchists, and the Golden Dawn member quickly ran out of the studio. The presenter, stupefied and frozen, sat with a look of disappointment. "You have invited fascists in here," one of them yelled, followed by a united chant that went on for several minutes: "Cops, TV, neo-Nazi—all the scum work together. We stand with immigrants; deport the cops and neo-Nazis."

The presenter stood up, his dapper blue jacket doused in white yogurt, and wiped his face as the activists left him with a final chant: "Fascist scum, you'll be hanged."

The presenter later said—with an overdramatic zeal that was laughable—that they had "suffered an attack." But, with varying effectiveness, force and direct confrontation have been corner-stone tactics in the fight against the Golden Dawn and other groups like it.

In December 2012, the Informal Anarchist Federation, a small anti-fascist group, released a communique claiming responsibility for a dynamite attack on a Golden Dawn office.[4] "We decided to hit Golden Dawn's offices because we believe that you have to hit out at Fascists first, before they hit you," the group said.

In November of the following year, the Militant People's Revolutionary Forces, an anarchist group, claimed responsibility for the killing of two Golden Dawn members as revenge for the murder of anti-fascist rapper Pavlos Fyssas a month earlier.[5] The statement cited ties between police—"armed dogs of the regime"—and the Golden Dawn, the former of which claimed fear of an impending attack on police targets owing to the rhetoric.[6] The claims of police collaboration with the neofascist party, however, were founded in fact. The *New York Times* reported on October 30, 2013, that an internal police investigation found at least ten officers to be linked to the party and to have "direct or indirect involvement with the criminal activities of the Golden Dawn."[7]

Fyssas's murder was a turning point for the broad anti-fascist left in Greece. The Golden Dawn had always met dedicated resistance to its violent attacks on migrants, leftists, critics, and journalists, but the fatal stabbing of a left-wing rapper in public was kerosene to the anti-fascist fire that had long burned in many Greeks' hearts.

Keerfa's Constantinou recalled the streets exploding with anger in the wake of the killing. It followed years of escalating violence by Golden Dawn's black-clad cadres and a number of less-known but equally significant incidents. Sitting in his office two weeks before the fourth anniversary of Fyssas's murder, he said the Golden Dawn had attempted to build paramilitary-like forces in the streets in the run-up to the attack. "It was a show of power there . . . but it was very clear that the central leadership of the Golden Dawn was organizing all these attacks," he remembered. "The police were there, and they did nothing."

A week of strikes, protests, and clashes with the neofascists and the police followed, with tens of thousands of angry Greeks mobilizing against the Golden Dawn in the wake of the murder. "This is not a political party . . . it's a Nazi, criminal group. We cannot accept them in the democratic spectrum because they are not democratic," Constantinou argued, adding that Fyssas was targeted because "he was openly anti-fascist in his music."

As I will explain later, murdering Fyssas, however, proved to be a strategic disaster for the neo-Nazis.

AN ANTI-FASCIST STRUGGLE FOR REFUGEES

As thousands of refugees and migrants continued to be turned away at borders in late 2015, a steady flow of new faces poured into the Notara solidarity center in the Exarchia.[8] Notara was founded in late September that year when around twenty anarchists occupied an abandoned, three-story building belonging to the Greek Ministry of Labor. The center provided temporary accommodation, basic medical treatment, clothing, and information for up to 130 refugees and migrants each day. It was one of several similar projects springing up across the country during the refugee crisis that continues to grip Europe. Tucked away in an alley with graffiti-lined walls, Notara was part of a network of activist-administered refugee solidarity centers in the neighborhood.

According to the UNHCR, more than a million refugees and migrants reached European shores by boat in 2015. With the doors open to welcome newcomers, enthusiasm was high as dozens of activists and volunteers debated how to expand their operations during an assembly meeting on a chilly night in early December 2015.

"We need more squats in places like Thessaloniki," one volunteer argued, referring to the coastal city in northern Greece that has become a stopping-off point along the refugee trail as people fleeing violence and economic despair look for safety and stability in Europe.

Mimi, a thirty-four-year-old anarchist and member of the squat, declined to provide her last name, fearing legal retribution. "We decided to do something in Athens about the refugee crisis," she told me, crushing the butt of her cigarette into an ashtray and swiftly lighting another.

The volunteers at the shelter included teachers, social workers, doctors, and full-time activists, among others, all united by a belief that the Greek government had failed to shoulder its responsibilities toward refugees. "We are against the state and we think the government has done nothing to provide a real solution," she said, adding that more than seventeen hundred refugees and migrants had stopped over in Notara between September 25 and December 1 of that year.

Most of the founding volunteers had been active in solidarity work on Greek islands over the summer of 2015, helping the thousands of people disembarking from boats and dinghies each day. "We had a full summer of experience under our belts and felt that refugees needed a safe space when they get to Athens, especially as the weather gets worse. From Athens, they still have a long journey ahead of them."

Deeply ideological, Notara rejected the philanthropic approach in favor of refugee solidarity. Refugees are asked to participate in the twice-weekly assembly meetings, where decisions are made through consensus. "The act of squatting in this building was a message to the government: It is failing everywhere, and we are putting a spotlight on it," she said. "We are anti-authoritarians. We reject the assistance of the state, NGOs, charities, and businesses."

She said that Notara is for "political people" and not for those whose sole motivations are humanitarian. "There is a difference between philanthropy and solidarity. We understand that we are on the same level as refugees."

"This is a project by the people. We believe that these are the key principles of self-organization, and we want to take the struggle into our own hands."

Exarchia itself is a symbolic choice. With virtually no government presence, the neighborhood is a hotbed of leftist and antiauthoritarian political activity where locals have clashed with police who try to encroach on their space. In late November 2016, Notara witnessed a surge of refugees and migrants after Macedonia sealed its borders to people who could not prove citizenship in Syria, Iraq, or Afghanistan, deeming those from other countries as "economic migrants." Macedonian president Gjorge Ivanov claimed that the presence of more than two thousand refugees in his country at any given time would result in "permanent and direct threats for national security."

Croatia, Slovenia, Serbia, and other countries quickly imposed similar measures. By March 2016, those borders would be totally sealed for refugees and migrants. Seraphim Seferiades, a political science professor at Panteion University in Athens, argued that the leftist Syriza government's about-face over Greece's debt crisis led to a vacuum on the left. "The response of the whole left—not just anarchists—has been quite amazing," he said. "People had accumulated so much energy to participate in politics and in domestic struggles in recent years, like the debt crisis, but all that energy went into the refugee solidarity initiative after the Syriza sellout."

Seferiades said that right-wing groups such as the Golden Dawn have been unable to capitalize on the refugee crisis so far. But if refugee solidarity activists are unable to tie their activism to Greece's domestic struggles, he warned, the hardline rightists could seize the opportunity. "It will eventually happen if the solidarity movement cannot continue to politicize the issue. They need to show the general population that what migrants and refugees are going through now is linked to the same European Union policies that make [Greeks] suffer."

Even volunteers' duties were divided up according to ideological principles, Mimi explained. "Only doing one job—like clothing distribution—can create a de facto hierarchy."

When they are not seeing patients, doctors distribute blankets and clothes to refugees whose suitcases were soaked or ruined during the perilous boat ride. Teachers do laundry and cook in between classes in Notara's preschool. Every few nights, a handful of activists ventured to Athens's Victoria Square—a gathering point for refugees—to bring those with nowhere to sleep back to the squat. Said, a twenty-one-year-old Moroccan who did not want to give his last name, left his hometown of Casablanca in early September. Braving the wintry Aegean waters and the lengthy land route, he made it to Idomeni on the Greek-Macedonian border, only to find that the crossing was closed for him. The closure created a buildup of tens of thousands of people in Greece, including those fleeing Morocco, Iran, Yemen, Eritrea, Somalia, Tunisia, and elsewhere.

Arriving back in Victoria Square, Said was approached by activists from Notara. "They told me there was a safe and warm place to sleep," he said. "I've been here for a few weeks. I don't know if the borders will open for us again."

Achilles Peklaris, an Exarchia-based journalist and anarchist activist, argued that Notara "is far more organized than the camps run by the government," accusing the state of providing substandard living conditions for refugees and migrants. "When you mention the word 'anarchy,' most people think of chaos and disorder," he said. "But if your worldview depends on a leader to tell you what to do, then we feel sorry for you." Referring to the weekly assemblies and inclusive decision-making process, Peklaris added: "No authority doesn't mean no rules. This is a direct democracy in the purest sense of the term."

As the assembly meeting came to an end, a family of Afghan refugees arrived. Activists welcomed them in, and a translator explained that they could stay for however long they needed. Mimi and others took their bags to a room with two beds, bringing them blankets and clean clothes. Pointing out the worsening weather and the closing of borders across the Balkans, she predicted that the coming months would be increasingly difficult. "With the borders closing, so many people are being sent back to Athens," Mimi said. "What are these people supposed to do? Sleep outside?"

HOTEL OCCUPATION

The roar of children's laughter erupted as they played tag and chased one another through the corridors, while several adults prepared the tables in the City Plaza hotel's dining hall in preparation to break the fast for Ramadan, a holy month for Muslims.[9] Tucked away down a side street in the Greek capital, the previously deserted hotel was occupied by left-wing Greek activists and turned into a squat for nearly four hundred refugees and migrants—half of them children—in late April 2016.

Sitting in the hotel's café, Lina Theodorou, a twenty-seven-year-old Athens-based lawyer and member of the Solidarity Initiative for Political and Economic Refugees, explained that they decided to occupy the hotel after border closures across the Balkans in March of that year. The hotel became home to Syrian and Afghan refugees and, to a lesser extent, families who fled Iraq, the occupied Palestinian territories, and several countries across Africa. The squat was administered by the refugees themselves, as well as between thirty and forty solidarity activists who volunteered informally on a daily basis. "We wanted to demand this public space because the mayor tried to throw all of the refugees out of [Victoria Square]," Theodorou told me, referring to an area in central Athens that has become a meeting place for those hoping to continue their journey. "It was a gesture to reclaim the right of the visibility of refugees because we feel that [the Greek government] is trying to hide them on the outskirts of the city."

In City Plaza, families lived in hotel rooms and had access to refugee-run and activist-administered healthcare, education, and dining. Most residents play a role according to their own abilities. Sculpted on principles of self-organizing and democracy, decisions about the squat's operations and activities are made when a general consensus is reached through discussion and debate between the residents and activists.

Wael Alfarawan, a twenty-six-year-old father of two and Palestinian refugee who fled Syria's Deraa, volunteered for months as a barber in the hotel. A group of children gather around as a young man sits in the chair and asks Wael to trim his beard. "We feel like one family here," he said as he turned on his clippers. "I contacted several NGOs and nobody helped me. They helped me a lot here [at City Plaza]. They help us, and we help each other."

Theodorou argued that refugee response initiatives have to be politicized in order to make a tangible difference. "We are leftists and anarchists—and we want to change the system that creates inequalities and this kind of refugee crisis," she said. "We are anticapitalist; we are against imperialism and great stuff like that. We believe that if your action doesn't connect with real-life improvement . . . it's an empty gesture."

With the Greek government's efforts to register asylum applicants stalling, anger and tensions had been growing in the camps. In the Greek islands, more than eighty-four hundred refugees and migrants were barred from traveling to mainland Greece without police permission until their applications were processed.

Rabee Abo Tarah, a twenty-six-year-old Syrian, worked in City Plaza as a translator for residents who don't speak English or Greek. He worked in Istanbul for a period and sent money back to his family in Damascus, but decided to move to Europe when his father died. After spending a month staying with people who opened their doors in Athens, activists informed him of the City Plaza squat. "This is a good project," he told me. "It is the occupation of a building towards political and humanitarian goals. I support it."

Thirty-seven-year-old Abdoulaziz Sall, a chef in the squat, left Senegal for Greece back in 2010, long before the eruption of the present refugee crisis rattling Europe. Living in nearby Exarchia, Sall volunteered at the hotel five days a week. As we sat together on a balcony, a steady chorus of pots and pans clanked behind us in the hotel's kitchen. Explaining that he was inspired by a sense of solidarity with people making the same journey he made six years ago, he said: "I quit my job and now I do full-time solidarity work. For me, my project is to help as much as possible."

In the squat's kitchen, a group of women and men chatted in Arabic and Dari as they prepared food for *iftar*, the meal with which Muslims break their fast each day during Ramadan. A man whistles softly while watching over a steel pot of coffee boiling on the stovetop. Nasim Lomani, a thirty-five-year-old member of the Solidarity Initiative who fled Afghanistan as a child, sat in the café and lit a cigarette. He said the squat's location is significant because the Greek government has tried to restrict the movement of asylum seekers, attempting to coerce them to relocate to official camps. "The camps have two very clear-cut features: All of them are outside of the city, in the middle of nowhere, with no access to social services," Lomani said. "The other thing is that almost all of them have tents."

"We wanted to set a good example of housing in order to say no to the way they are building the camps," he concluded. "There is an alternative—treating [refugees] like humans."

"BEGINNING OF THE END FOR FASCISM"

The murder of Pavlos Fyssas was a turning point for both the far right and their opponents.

In September 2017, when I visited the Fyssas home, his mother Magda walked to the corner of her living room and lit four crimson-colored candles. She placed them next to a smaller, already-lit white candle under a large charcoal sketch of her son. In the memory-filled home she said has felt empty since the loss of her son, she did this every day.[10]

The murder of thirty-four-year-old Fyssas on September 18, 2013, ignited weeks of anti-fascist protests, clashes with riot police, and altercations with Golden Dawn, the neofascist party that holds seventeen seats in Greece's parliament. Protesters rally in cities across the country every year on the anniversary of his death, mourning Pavlos and other victims of far-right violence. His murder was a galvanizing moment for the anti-fascist movement, which has since elevated Pavlos, whose rap name was Killah P, to martyr status.

In the working-class neighborhood of Keratsini, a large monument depicting Pavlos rapping sits not far from his mother's home. Throughout Athens, Piraeus, and elsewhere, his name was tagged on buildings and sidewalks, his face emblazoned on posters.

Magda's living room was her personal shrine to Pavlos, the wall covered in photos, posters, and paintings of him. In one photo, Pavlos wore a billowy black wig for Apokries, a Greek holiday akin to Halloween. In another, he squats with crossed arms and mimics the American hip-hop group Run DMC, wearing a white jumpsuit and a large gold chain. In a drawer under the photos, Magda keeps Pavlos's letters and journal entries. She shuffles through the papers silently until she finds the one she is searching for: an entry titled "Alcoholic Anthology."

"If all of your life is eaten away by fear of the familiar and unfamiliar," the hand-written entry reads, "then death will find you fearful and sweaty, floundering and begging for mercy and more time, still harboring the illusion that something might change at the last moment."

Magda spoke comfortably about the political implications of her son's murder and boldly about Golden Dawn, the members of which she described plainly as "neo-Nazis" and "criminals." Yet, when asked about Pavlos's character, her mood turned somber and her expression severe.

"You're asking a mother about what kind of a person her son was," she said, her voice growing shaky. She paused, lit a cigarette, took a deep draw from it and, after a few moments, settled on a description of her son: "He was a free man."

Pavlos spent the hours leading up to his murder in a café with a group of friends, among them his partner, watching a local football match on television. After they left the café to head for another, an altercation occurred. The exact details of the incident remain disputed, but police were called to the scene. Pavlos had been stabbed. He was taken to a hospital, where he later died. His family, friends, and some witnesses say that a group of far-rightists confronted Pavlos and his companions. Pavlos fought them off while his friends escaped, they say. Magda learned that her son had been injured from Pavlos's father. She rushed to the hospital, where a doctor told her that he had died of stab wounds. "I didn't want to believe [it]," she said softly.

Giorgos Roupakias, who worked in the cafeteria at a Golden Dawn office and publicized his support for the party, was arrested for the murder. He later admitted to killing Pavlos. In 2016, he was released from pretrial detention and placed under house arrest. Golden Dawn denied any direct connection with the incident, although Nikolaos Michaloliakos, the founder and leader of the party, stated that his party accepts "political responsibility" for the murder.

"With regards to political responsibility for the murder of Fyssas in Keratsini, we accept it," he said during a 2015 radio interview.[11] "As for criminal liability, there isn't any. Is it right to condemn a whole party because one of its followers carried out a condemnable act?"

In the months leading up to his death, Pavlos and his mother had regularly discussed the rise of Golden Dawn, which had transformed from an obscure band of hardliners flirting with Nazi imagery to a parliamentary party equipped with a paramilitary carrying out raids and attacks in neighborhoods with a large number of immigrants. Just a year earlier, in 2012, Golden Dawn entered the Greek parliament for the first time after securing twenty-one parliamentary seats and some 7 percent of the vote.

The sudden explosion of support for the party sent chills through much of Greek society, including the Fyssas family.

While walking together in their historically left-wing neighborhood four months before the murder, Magda and Pavlos witnessed a flag-flying motorcade of Golden Dawn members parading through Keratsini. "We didn't feel safe," she remembers, crushing a cigarette into an ashtray she balances in her lap. "We knew something bad was on the way, but I couldn't have imagined it would impact my family directly."

Following Pavlos's murder, police arrested sixty-nine Golden Dawn members, including the party's senior leadership, who were subsequently charged with operating a criminal organization. Electra Alexandropoulou of Golden Dawn Watch, a group that monitors the party, said the trial will determine the future of the party and whether its offices and operations will eventually be shuttered. The bulk of the evidence suggested that the attack on Pavlos—as well as similar attacks on immigrants and political opponents—were carried out with the knowledge and approval of high-ranking Golden Dawn officials.

If those in the senior cadre aren't eventually convicted, she argued, the court will send the message that Golden Dawn enjoys impunity. "If you know someone has coordinated a murder and you let him go free, what message are you giving him? That he's welcome to do it again."

Sitting in his fifth-floor office, Petros Constantinou recalls the moment a fellow activist called to inform him of Pavlos's death.

Constantinou and other left-wing organizers sprang into action. The local media was reporting that the killing was the result of a football rivalry, but within five hours Keerfa and a broad alliance of left-wing groups had released a statement pointing the finger at Golden Dawn. Weeks of demonstrations ensued, with tens of thousands of Greeks swarming streets across the country, particularly in the capital. "For us, it was very clear," Constantinou said. "We don't let the Nazis have any space in the streets, in the media, in the parliament, anywhere."

Protests turned into violent clashes with the police. Golden Dawn's opponents demanded the immediate closure of the party. "This is not a political party," Constantinou said. "This is a Nazi, criminal group ... and we cannot accept them as part of a democratic [system] because they don't respect democracy."

Just weeks after the murder of Pavlos, gunmen shot and killed two Golden Dawn members outside the party's office in the Neo Irakleio area of the capital. Commemorations of the murder of Pavlos and the 2008 police killing of fifteen-year-old Alexis Grigoropoulos serve as "forms of communication" for anti-fascists and the broader antiauthoritarian movement, said Nicholas Apoifis, the author of *Anarchy in Athens*. "It's quite a legitimate mourning of the past," he explained. "But there is no way to get around the fact that the images of Fyssas and Grigoropoulos are used to convey ... anger and to galvanize the [anti-fascist] space. They are ways of articulating politics, of articulating resistance and of articulating emotional responses to events as well."

It has been more than two years since the start of the Golden

Dawn trial, which involves sixty-nine defendants and will eventually rule on the legality of the organization itself. Slated to conclude in late 2018, it has progressed slowly, largely owing to the complexity of the case. More than eleven hundred documents about alleged crimes committed by party members and officials are being examined during the trial, while hundreds of witnesses testified. Many of the testimonies painted a picture of premeditated violence by Golden Dawn members, and some witnesses touched all too close to home for the Fyssas family. "The knives will come out after the elections," one party member said, according to the testimony of filmmaker Konstantinos Georgousis, who followed party candidates during the run-up to the 2012 elections in the documentary *The Cleaners*.[12]

Earlier in the trial, Violetta Kougatsou, who testified as a witness to Pavlos's murder, told the jury that police were already present at the time of the attack: "Pavlos died helplessly, killed in front of the police. These policemen did not represent the Greek people."

Police provided varying explanations of the night's events, some of which purport that officers were unable to intervene because of a mob of club-wielding far-rightists who had assembled and others of which claim the officers arrived after the stabbing took place.

Javed Aslam left Pakistan and immigrated to Greece in 1996, when he said there was little anti-immigrant violence in the streets. Occasionally slapping the wooden desk in front of him in his Athens office when I met him in September 2017, Aslam recalled the explosion of violence that hit the Pakistani migrant laborer community between 2010 and 2013. Behind Aslam, the president of the Pakistani Community in Greece, a union for migrant workers, was a sticker. "Smash the neo-Nazis," it read in Greek.

He recalled scenes of violence from that period: Golden Dawn members would enter buses full of Pakistani laborers and assault them in broad daylight, he said, adding that such attacks rarely elicited a response from Greeks or the media.

In January 2013, nine months before Pavlos was killed, a pair of assailants affiliated with Golden Dawn stabbed to death Shahzad Luqman, a twenty-six-year-old Pakistani who was on his way to work. "This was a very, very difficult day . . . [for all] immigrant communities—not just Pakistanis," Aslam said. "That was when you saw that no one is going to help you. . . . People were thinking that no one is safe here, that there [are] no laws and rights for immigrants."

Facing political pressure and criminal charges that could render the organization extinct, Golden Dawn subsequently attempted to rebrand its image as a legitimate nationalist party, abandoning many of the public displays of Nazi-like salutes and scaling back street-level violence. The attacks never came to a complete standstill, though, and the influx of tens of thousands of refugees and migrants in recent years was accompanied by a wave of violence targeting camps and asylum seekers.

On the island of Chios, antirefugee violence quickly became part and parcel of life in the refugee camps after the mass influx of displaced people that started in 2015. In May of 2017, an unspecified number of alleged Golden Dawn members beat and injured dozens of Pakistani laborers in Aspropyrgos, located near the capital, according to local media reports.[13]

For Aslam, the murders of Pavlos and Shahzad represented a turning point in the struggle against Golden Dawn while providing a shared rallying cry for Greeks and immigrants alike. "If we [don't] remember them, it means we will let them down," he argued. "They give us [a way] to be together in the fight against fascism. The murders of Fyssas and [Luqman were] the beginning of the end for fascism."

Athanasios Perrakis, a thirty-four-year-old Greek rapper whose stage name is Tiny Jackal, was in the E-13 hip-hop crew with Pavlos and one of his best friends. On a warm September afternoon, I joined him as he hopped in his silver SUV and set off from his native Keratsini for Athens. The American rapper Big Pun blared through his sound system. On his left arm were tattoos of his favorite rap artists: 2Pac, Run DMC, Redman, and others. On his hand were Pavlos's logo and the date of his death. "This is so I don't forget," he said. He weaved through Keratsini's narrow back alleyways, passing graffiti of the hammer and sickle, anti-fascist declarations, and calls for working-class revolution. Once in Athens, he stopped at a red light near a crowded intersection. Plastered on a wall were posters announcing two demonstrations.

The first was slated for September 16 outside the U.S. embassy in Athens and bore Pavlos's face superimposed next to that of an American anti-fascist who was murdered by a neo-Nazi in Charlottesville, Virginia, in August 2017. "Four years since the murder of Pavlos Fyssas," it read. "One month since the murder of Heather Heyer in the U.S. From Greece to America, smash the neo-Nazis." The other was to be held September 18. "Close the offices of the neo-Nazis," it proclaimed.

Athanasios recalled his last meeting with Pavlos, a few days before he was killed. They discussed creating a Piraeus-based crew that would function as a Greek rendition of the Wu-Tang Clan. After the murder, Athanasios recorded a tribute album for Pavlos. But after being accused of profiting from his friend's death, he retreated into depression for a while. Four years later, he still struggled with the loss. He described being overwhelmed with emotions when he heard Pavlos's songs blasting from a passing car or saw images of his friend on the walls of his hometown. One of Pavlos's songs—titled "Zoria," which translates imprecisely to "hard times"—continued to haunt him.

> A day like this is a good one to die,
> Gracefully and on public display.
> My name is Pavlos Fyssas from Piraeus,
> Greek—whatever that means,
> Not a flag, a black-shirted
> Spawn of Achilles and Karaiskakis.

For Athanasios, these lyrics suggested that Pavlos suspected he might be killed by neofascists, who are notorious for dressing in black and waving Greek flags. He points to Golden Dawn's ultranationalism and the view that they carry the legacies of Greek mythological heroes like Achilles and nationalist figures such as Georgios Karaiskakis, the military leader who commanded battalions in the fight against Ottoman rule in the nineteenth century.

In the days and weeks leading up to the killing, Athanasios said tensions hit a fever pitch in Keratsini. Among the clashes between anti-fascists and Golden Dawn members that are still seared into his memory is an instance in which the latter beat a group of communist union organizers for hanging anti-fascist posters in the neighborhood.

Emphasizing the political nature of the violence, Athanasios nonetheless said he regretted the widespread reduction of Pavlos to an anti-fascist musician. "So many people focus on the songs about his anti-fascist actions," he says, frustrated. "Pavlos was not only that, although he was [an anti-fascist]. He had songs about friendship, family, life, and what to do with society. He was the type of person who would help you with anything."

Back in her home, Magda said her family would continue to fight despite feeling that no legal measures will provide justice for the loss of her son. "What we do is for everyone who is still out there," she maintained. "Like we lost Pavlos, someone else may be killed in the same way."

She concluded: "Pavlos died as a free man who tried to kill fear that night. . . . He stayed back to defend his friends, and he may have known that it would cost him his life."

She lit another cigarette and pointed again to her son's journal entry sitting on the coffee table. "Never underestimate the heart of a free man," the note exclaimed. "I hope for nothing, I fear nothing, and I am free. This is exactly why I am not afraid to die now—because I will keep on living, and that's your biggest fear."

At the bottom, it read: "To be continued."

PUNCHING BACK

On an early September evening in 2017, just weeks before the anniversary of Fyssas's death, people were trickling into the half-basement of an old gray apartment block in the Greek capital.[14] Once inside, they removed their shoes and disappeared into locker rooms before reemerging to take their spot on the padded blue-and-red floor. A guttural German punk song blared from the speakers. A black flag hung beside the bathroom door. "The genuine anti-fascist fighting club," it read.

Founded by thirty-nine-year-old anarchist Ilias Lamprou, the White Tiger Muay Thai Camp was one of the first anti-fascist gyms to take root in Athens.

Barefoot and wearing a gray hoodie with cut-off sleeves over a faded black shirt, Lamprou directed his forty or so novice students as they warmed up. "Faster," he urged them, speaking over a litany of grunts as fists and legs thudded against punching bags. His hair was short, neat, and peppered with gray. A scatter of tattoos on his arms and legs, he stood cross-armed as he issued directions.

Earlier in the day, Lamprou sat at his cluttered desk in the gym's office. On the wall were photos of him competing in Muay Thai tournaments, fists raised as he posed with fellow fighters and students. White Tiger applied the political philosophies of self-organization and antiauthoritarianism to martial arts.

He recalled how, when he was twenty years old, a friend advised him to start Muay Thai training. But what began for "practical reasons"—a need to defend himself from the police ("ACAB," the acronym for "all cops are bastards," is emblazoned on a banner that hangs from the gym's ceiling) and Golden Dawn—became a passion. "I started Muay Thai, and I loved it," he recalled, adding that the martial art was still relatively unknown in Greece at the time. "You can't avoid falling in love with it. . . . I tried and loved it from the first time. So, I continued."

Lamprou has been involved in anarchist activism for more than two decades. In Greece, he has participated in rallies in solidarity with political prisoners worldwide and against the far right, police brutality, and economic austerity. In 2010, along with other activists, he sailed toward the Gaza Strip in a fleet of six civilian ships that hoped to break Israel's ongoing siege of the coastal enclave where nearly two million Palestinians reside. During that incident, Israeli forces raided the flotillas, killing nine activists on the *Mavi Marmara*, one of the ships.

During the raid, Lamprou was aboard the *Free Mediterranean* ship, which was boarded by Israeli soldiers who used rubber-coated steel bullets, tear gas, and electric shocks before detaining the passengers.

In 2001, he attended massive antiglobalization protests in

Genoa, Italy, and has joined solidarity trips to Palestinian refugee camps in Lebanon, where tens of thousands of people live in gruesome conditions and endure institutional discrimination. Lamprou has also traveled to Thailand several times for Muay Thai training.

Searching for a way to combine his activism with his passion for Muay Thai, Lamprou decided to establish White Tiger by drawing on the popular tradition of anti-fascist sports clubs and training spaces in other European countries. "I have a long history in the [anarchist] movement," he explained. "I couldn't keep those [political commitments] outside the gym."

At the time White Tiger was established, Greece was in the midst of a sharp surge in far-right violence, much of which targeted refugees and migrants, whom the far right scapegoated for the country's economic woes. In the run-up to that year's elections, after which the neofascist party first entered parliament, the Greek economic crisis fueled street battles between anti-fascists and the Golden Dawn. Lamprou said there was an urgent need for gyms that provide practical training in self-defense while reflecting the political worldview of the anti-fascist movement. "After the big boom of Golden Dawn, it was a necessity in Greece [to create] self-organized gyms, and gyms that keep out fascists and the cops," Lamprou said, explaining that many other gyms at the time were frequented by police officers and far-rightists. Clasping his hands together as he recalled those turbulent times, he continued: "There was a purely practical [reason]: We own the streets, and we want to keep them ours."

Lamprou also argued that martial arts demand respect for opponents and those who are different from you. "That's why we cannot give martial arts to the fascists."

White Tiger had more than 120 students spread across three skill levels—beginner, novice, and expert—many of whom participate in competitions as a team and attend training sessions several times a week. Among them were Greeks, internationals from across Europe and North America, and migrants and refugees from places such as Syria, Iraq, and Afghanistan. The top level includes some thirty people, known as the fighting team, who participated in competitions in Greece and abroad twice a month.

Thannasis K, a twenty-two-year-old Greek, was a Muay Thai novice at the time I met him. "I'm living in an area of Athens that has had a lot of racist attacks and attacks against anarchists," he said, wiping sweat from his brow as he stood outside the gym after practice. "So, I wanted to start an art of fighting ... and know how to defend [myself] in the street in a fight."

Thannasis explained that he left his previous gym after he learned that Lamprou refused to put his fighters in the ring against an opponent who was being cheered on by Ilias Kasidiaris, a Golden Dawn member and parliamentarian. "You must have solidarity [and] anti-fascism in your whole life, so it's very important to have this also in a place where you learn martial arts," he said.

Back in the gym, a group of students sparred in the boxing ring. For Lamprou, the rejection of patriarchy is one of the most important features of White Tiger's approach to athleticism. Attendees who engage in sexist or patriarchal behavior are kicked out. "Antisexism is part of our life," he said. "It's not an ideology; it's a way of life."

Around half of the White Tiger's weekly participants are female, and Lamprou says his female competitive squad is "the best in Greece."

"If any macho guy comes, he'll see that the environment isn't good for him," he continued.

Drawing on the anti-fascist notion of denying platforms for racists and fascists, Lamprou says he will not put his fighters in the ring to compete with opponents who are known Golden Dawn affiliates or supporters. "We can't compete with [fascists]," he explained. "In Muay Thai, there is a lot of respect for the opponent. You can't pay respect to a fascist."

The streets, he said, are where the far right ought to be confronted. White Tiger is part of a broader culture of anti-fascism in Greece, specifically in the Athenian neighborhood of Exarchia where it is located.

Author and researcher Nicholas Apoifis explained that the "collective memory of literal fascism" in Greece has fostered a long tradition of anti-fascism that places a special emphasis on direct confrontation. In 1941, during the Second World War, Nazi Germany, Mussolini's Italy, and fascist-allied Bulgaria occupied Greece. By the time they were expelled in 1944, nearly sixty thousand Greek Jews had been killed. Anti-fascist resistance was widespread during that period. Between 1967 and 1974, Greece was ruled by far-right military juntas. A mass uprising at the Athens polytechnic school led to a series of events that resulted in that regime's collapse. "There is a history of anti-fascism more broadly in Greece because of the history of fascism: the massacres of communists, the torture of anarchists, and the massacres of social democrats," Apoifis explained. "There is a rich history in the face of fascism and resistance to that."

Apoifis pointed to a 1984 incident as one of the most crucial historical moments in the contemporary anti-fascist movement in Greece. In December of that year, thousands of anarchists and far-leftists assembled in Athens and employed black bloc tactics during confrontations at the Hotel Caravel, where a far-right conference headlined by French populist Jean-Marie Le Pen was taking place. While researching his book, Apoifis said he observed a commitment among anti-fascists to defend by force those areas where they maintain a strong presence. "It's a calculated political project. It's another form of direct action. They're having discussions about it, but they are also going out and implementing their politics."

Although Lamprou had yet to personally use his Muay Thai skills to confront Golden Dawn members, he said it has often come in handy at demonstrations where clashes with riot police break out. "Twenty years ago, you couldn't find fascists in Athens," he recalled. "But the necessity became real because we all of the sudden had fascists outside doing patrols."

Lamprou rejected the idea that gyms should be apolitical spaces. "The mentality here is that we can't divide athleticism

from politics," he concluded. "I've been in the anarchist movement for the last twenty years. I've been in Palestine, Lebanon,
Genoa, Athens ... in all the big [protests]. Antisexism, anti-fascism—we couldn't live any other way, whether it's in the gym or
in our workplace."

NOTES

1. Patrick Strickland, "From NATO to Antifa: One Afghan's Journey to
Greece," *Al Jazeera English*, May 23, 2017, http://www.aljazeera.com/indepth/
features/2017/04/nato-antifa-afghan-journey-greece-170424034117957.html.

2. Karolina Tagaris, "Racist Attacks in Greece Hit 'Alarming' Levels:
UNHCR," *Reuters*, October 23, 2012, http://www.reuters.com/article/us-gree
ce-violence-idUSBRE89M12R20121023.

3. "Antifa Yogurt Attack during Live TV News show (Greece)," YouTube
video, April 6, 2012, https://www.youtube.com/watch?v=pONziL6fR4o.

4. Andy Dabilis, "Anti-fascists Claim Golden Dawn Bombing," *Greek Reporter*, December 8, 2012, http://greece.greekreporter.com/2012/12/08/anti-
fascists-claim-golden-dawn-bombing/.

5. Mitch Sweson, "Anarchists Are Killing Neo-Nazis in Greece," *Medium*,
War Is Boring, November 21, 2013, https://medium.com/war-is-boring/anar
chists-are-killing-neo-nazis-in-greece-baca262397da.

6. "Greek Police on High Alert amid Fears of New Terror Hit," *Ekathimerini*,
November 18, 2013, http://www.ekathimerini.com/155566/article/ekathime
rini/news/greek-police-on-high-alert-amid-fears-of-new-terror-hit.

7. Niki Kitsantonis, "Greek Police Say 10 Officers Have Links to Golden
Dawn," *New York Times*, October 30, 2013, http://www.nytimes.com/2013/10/
31/world/europe/greek-police-say-10-officers-have-links-to-golden-dawn
.html.

8. Patrick Strickland, "Greek Anarchists Organise for Refugees as 'State Fails,'" *Al Jazeera English*, January 19, 2016, http://www.aljazeera.com/in depth/features/2016/01/greek-anarchists-organise-refugees-state-fails-16 0117032251199.html.

9. Patrick Strickland, "Greek Leftists Turn Deserted Hotel into Refugee Homes," *Al Jazeera English*, July 3, 2016, http://www.aljazeera.com/indepth/features/2016/06/greek-leftists-turn-deserted-hotel-refugee-homes-16062 9131217044.html.

10. Patrick Strickland, "Greece Mourns Slain Anti-fascist Rapper Pavlos Fyssas," *Al Jazeera English*, September 15, 2017, http://www.aljazeera.com/in depth/features/2017/09/greece-mourns-slain-anti-fascist-rapper-pavlos-fyssas-170911080142110.html.

11. Melpomeni Maragkidou, "A Neo-Nazi Political Party in Greece Has Accepted Responsibility for the Murder of an Antifascist Rapper," *Vice*, September 18, 2015, https://www.vice.com/en_au/article/xd7v4a/golden-dawn-accepts-political-responsibility-for-murder-876.

12. "Day 156: The Knives Will Come Out after the Elections," Golden Dawn Watch, May 28, 2017, http://goldendawnwatch.org/?p=3116&lang=en.

13. Patrick Strickland, "Protests Planned after Pakistani Migrants Attacked," *Al Jazeera English*, October 12, 2017, http://www.aljazeera.com/news/2017/10/protests-planned-pakistani-migrants-attacked-17101111242 0238.html.

14. Patrick Strickland, "Punching Back: Greek Gym Trains for Anti-fascist Action," *Al Jazeera English*, September 19, 2017, http://www.aljazeera.com/in depth/features/2017/09/punching-greek-gym-trains-anti-fascist-action-170 911085404277.html.

SLOVAKIA

When Ján Benčík's son created a Facebook profile for him after he retired in 2012, he saw little reason to log on save for boredom.[1] A little more than a year ago, however, he discovered a way to make social media feel worthwhile: tracking, exposing, and doxing neofascist politicians and activists and others on the far right.

On a frigid afternoon in early March 2017, the sixty-eight-year-old stepped into the local pizza parlor and shook snow off his winter coat as he removed and hung it on a rack. He found an empty seat on an earth-toned sofa in the corner of the room, removed his laptop from its case, and flipped it open.

The onetime phone technician and publishing house employee opened a folder on his desktop, then clicked on screenshot after screenshot of social media posts—most of them deleted by now —written by far-right users, among them politicians and leading activists. Benčík pointed to the screen, which displayed a hefty Slovak man donning a backward baseball cap and grinning widely as he lies on an oven in Poland's Auschwitz concentration camp. Sarcastically posing with his head in his hands, his arms were heavily tattooed with neo-Nazi imagery and coded numbers.

Benčík put photos like this one on the front page of his blog, where he dumps the personal information of people who post white supremacist and racist content on social media. Among those he has gone after are parliamentarians from Kotleba—Our

People's Slovakia Party (LSNS), a far-right party with neo-Nazi roots.

Since its founding in 2010, the LSNS was considered a ragtag band of inconsequential hardliners. That all changed in March 2016, however, when the party captured nearly 10 percent of the popular vote in national elections and secured fourteen seats in the National Council, Slovakia's parliament. The following day, thousands of people took to the streets to protest the LSNS and the "clerical fascism" they said the party represents.

"This is a protest against the fact that a clerical fascist party has made it into parliament. We lived through this once before, we do not want history to repeat itself. In addition to the [LSNS] openly espousing the clerical fascist legacy of the Slovak State and the war criminal Jozef Tiso, it also promotes hatred against all minorities, including people who hold minority opinions," Eva Riečanská, one of the rally's organizers, told Czech media in Bratislava.[2]

"Look at this one," Benčík said and motioned to the screen again, this time showing a status written by a LSNS parliamentarian. In both English and Slovak, it quoted the infamous hate slogan, written by American white supremacist David Lane, commonly referred to as "14 words": "We must secure the existence of our people and a future for white children."

He clicked the screen and another post came up: "Nothing will save us but killing all the Jews."

And again: "Slovakia is not Africa!"

In addition to tracking white supremacists and hate speech, Benčík has doxed Slovaks who trekked to eastern Ukraine to fight with pro-Russian militias.

His work has won him the respect of Slovakia's progressives, and even a meeting with the president. In the fall of 2016, one of the country's largest magazines published his face on the cover with the title "the fascist hunter." Yet the feedback has not been uniformly positive. Throughout the last year, far-right activists and Slovak mercenaries in Ukraine have sent him a slew of death threats. Far-right activists also prominently placed Benčík's name on a list of "opponents of the state."

Despite the death threats—among them detailed vows to stab him to death in the street and publicly hang him—Benčík told me he refused to be deterred. Nonetheless, he lived under police protection for several months, he conceded. "I can't give them the pleasure of [not blogging] about them," he explained. "It would be funny to be so afraid of men who just delete their statuses and profiles as soon as I write about them."

Since the LSNS made huge electoral gains in 2016, his work has assumed a heightened significance. "I lived for forty-one years under the communist regime, so I don't want to live the rest of my life under a neo-Nazi dictatorship," he said, "and I also don't want my children and grandchildren to live under them."

He bobbed his head lightly to the tune of the music drifting from the restaurant's speakers. "Come on, baby, do the loco-motion with me," he sings along softly, laughing. Switching back to the conversation, Benčík joked: "They are brave like Arnold Schwarzenegger and post photos from the gym. But when you write about them, they get scared and delete [their posts]."

NEOFASCISM IN LIGHT AND SHADE

The LSNS has roots in the now-banned Slovak Togetherness National Party, which was also headed by LSNS namesake and leader Marian Kotleba. In the past, LSNS members used to march through cities and towns in black uniforms modeled on those worn by the Hlinka Guard, the militia of the First Slovak Republic (1939–1945), a Nazi satellite state during the Second World War.

Kotleba, who was once a vocal neo-Nazi, had ostensibly ordered his underlings to trade the black garb for green shirts adorned with a double cross, the party's emblem. The virulently anti-Semitic rhetoric of Kotleba and his followers has now given way to fiercely anti-Roma incitement.

Many Slovaks don't trust Kotleba's promises that the party has no connection to neo-Nazism or neofascism. The LSNS platform refers to Roma as "social parasites" and "extremists" and expresses contempt for the European Union, the United States, NATO, and Israel. The LSNS has also preserved its commitment to hypernationalism, Christianity, and "moral preservation."

Keeping to its custom of not speaking to foreign reporters, the LSNS failed to reply to my numerous requests for an interview. The party's website said its "uncompromising program, open and striking rhetoric and the fight against parasites and thieves in the parliament and among people" motivates attacks "by foreign media" and government persecution.

Echoing Second World War–era fascist themes, it concluded: "Nevertheless, we are determined to sacrifice ourselves for Slovakia—For God . . . and the nation!"

Although the LSNS is not the sole actor in the crowded political terrain of Slovakia's far right, Kotleba's band of zealous followers has managed the most successful transition from the shadows into the corridors of power, at least to some extent.

The LSNS openly praised the First Slovak Republic, which, under the rule of Catholic priest and president Jozef Tiso, deported an estimated seventy-five thousand Jews, or 83 percent of the country's prewar Jewish population. Kotleba has described that republic as "like living in a heaven."

During the 2016 national elections, the party used a successful blend of online campaigning and visiting isolated and deprived communities enduring immense economic hardship. Although polls predicted the LSNS would clinch between 1.5 and 3 percent of the vote, nearly one of every ten voters cast a ballot for them. Many of their members are now legislators, and some of them sit on influential parliamentary committees such as the one dedicated to securing human rights in the country.

Alena Kluknavská, a postdoctoral researcher at Masaryk University in the neighboring Czech Republic, said the LSNS used a three-prong strategy to build its base while simultaneously eschewing traditional electoral campaigning. There were no LSNS television commercials, no rallies, and no images of Kotleba's face pasted on billboards. Instead, the LSNS focused on visiting poor communities, exploiting tensions between white Slovaks and Roma, and cultivating a following through "nationalist, xenophobic, and populist" sentiment in the online sphere, said Kluknavská.

Railing against Roma, Muslims, and other religious and ethnic minorities, the LSNS provided financial support to impoverished Slovak families living in communities feeling the pains of institutional deprivation. By "positioning itself as the advocate and defender of 'ordinary' people," Kluknavská argued, the LSNS has been able to sculpt a presence beyond the digital sphere, with a growing number of foot soldiers on the streets.

In April and May 2017, Facebook began clamping down on LSNS-affiliated accounts because of their violent and racist content.[3] The local *Denník N* daily reported that thirty-seven of the 140 profiles administered by or related to the party had been shut down. Within weeks, however, at least nine of those pages were back online.

A satirical page mocking the LSNS, entitled "Zomri" (Die), was also closed and remained offline after party members submitted mass complaints. The party's official page, which had about eighty thousand likes, was also removed in April that year.

"Through the page, and the dozens of others, LSNS voiced its negative stances about liberals, Roma, Muslims, homosexuals, Jews, and other groups that it is hostile to," reported the *Slovak Spectator* at the time.

In a poll of 102 university students, the LSNS was supported by roughly 10 percent. Yet analysts predicted that support could reach nearly one-third if the LSNS focused its message on leaving NATO and the EU.[4]

A year earlier, the bulk of LSNS support came from Slovaks aged between eighteen and twenty-nine. "It's safe to say that the idea of leaving the EU and NATO really attracts some 20 to 30 percent of students in general," said Pavol Baboš of the school of political sciences of Comenius University in Bratislava, explaining that the conspiracy theories that resonate with this demographic include the following: "The EU is damaging our agriculture, Brussels is dictating us everything, the NATO is controlled by Jews who want to gain power over the whole world."

ATTACKS AND INCITEMENT HAND IN HAND

In March 2016, just two weeks after the LSNS entered the parliament, one of the party's legislators showed up in parliament brandishing a firearm.[5] Upon passing through security, he handed over the nine-millimeter Grand Power pistol.[6]

Later, in June 2015, thousands of LSNS members and other far-rightists held an anti-Muslim rally in Bratislava. By the end of the day, participants had attacked a Saudi family, including a child in a stroller, pelting them with stones.

In March 2016, twenty-two-year-old LSNS legislator Milan Mazurek was caught on film hurling racist abuse at a group of Muslims in the capital.[7] As he and his comrades shouted insults referring to the sexuality of the women in the group, police were forced to intervene and help the frightened family escape. He shouted at them: "Allah [Arabic for 'God'] is Satan."

Mazurek was known for his rampant Holocaust denial. In one social media post, he wrote: "I do not advocate any regime, but regarding the Third Reich we only know lies and fairy tales about six million Jews and soap. Nothing but lies are taught about Hitler."[8] He wasn't prosecuted for those comments, although they violate the country's legal code.

A few days later, on March 22, 2016, unknown assailants attacked a Muslim woman of African descent at a bus stop in the capital. One tried to wrestle away her bag as another ripped off her veil. Local media reported that they had yelled "black," "dirty," and "Muslim" during the assault.

In February 2017, Mazurek and fellow LSNS parliamentarian Stanislav Mizík were issued fines of one thousand euros each after proclaiming in parliament that Islam is a "cruel, disgusting and inhumane political system" and the "satanic and pedophile work of the devil."[9]

In March 2017, Mazurek was prosecuted for racist remarks that violated the country's penal code.[10] "We don't need to pour 300 million euros for seven or eight years into just one community, to build playgrounds in the gypsy settlements so they can break the equipment, to build preschools so they can destroy them, we don't need to teach them to dance or to use a computer, we need to put them to work," Mazurek had said during an interview, using a derogatory slur for Roma. "150 million euros will be used just for houses in those gypsy settlements, for people who have made no contributions to our culture, to our nation, or to our state budget—exactly the opposite, they have decided to live an asocial lifestyle and have sucked our social welfare system dry."

SPECIAL HATRED OF ROMA

Roma, the ethnic minority who make up some 10 percent of the country's population at nearly a half-million people, are among the most vulnerable and oppressed groups in Slovakia. Systematically excluded from the labor market and confined to ghettoes, Roma suffer from an immense unemployment rate and vigilante violence, while enduring poor living conditions and an imposed dependency on state welfare services to survive.

On March 10, 2012, a pair of Roma boys, aged eleven and twelve, accidentally sparked a fire at fourteenth-century Krásna Hôrka Castle, situated in the mountainous region of eastern Slovakia. The historical structure sustained severe damage, including the destruction of its rooftop and three bells. The boys had set the castle on fire by accident while smoking a cigarette far from the watchful eyes of their parents and other adults in the nearby Roma slum where they lived. Acutely aware of the violence that targets their community on a regular basis, local Roma men organized and prepared to defend the area in case right-wing extremists arrived for blood.

The LSNS quickly seized the incident in what *Vice* described at the time as an equivalent of the German Reichstag fire, which served as a pretext for a deadly and lengthy political crackdown on opponents of Hitler's Nazi regime.[11]

During a demonstration a few months later, Kotleba, donning military garb, addressed an audience of around 150 people who had gathered amid anti-Roma furor. He roared:

> We don't like the way this government deprives polite people in order to improve the position of parasites.... This burned castle is a symbol of the way it will go if the government doesn't do anything with this growing and increasing menace.... If we don't do anything about it, the situation will continue getting worse.... If the state wasn't creating surprisingly good conditions for these Gypsy extremists, what do you think would happen? They would all go to England. They can go anywhere; they have freedom to move. If they suffer so much in Slovakia, no one is keeping them here. No one will miss them. I don't have to tell you that I wouldn't miss them at all.[12]

LSNS attendees told media that they sought to repeat the actions of Milan Juhász, an off-duty police officer who had killed and wounded five Roma.[13]

The relationship between the officer's murderous rampage and the rhetoric employed by LSNS, however, appears to have been symbiotic. The Kotleba outfit had campaigned for a "great cleansing" of Roma from the village of Krásnohorské Podhradie while regularly holding assemblies against "Roma oppression."[14]

The hate speech and the violence went together.

Many of Slovakia's political elite and liberal urban dwellers were shocked to wake up to the party's gains the day after the 2016 elections. But the signs of Kotleba's increasing strength were already present, analysts point out.

At the time, in the Banská Bystrica region, Kotleba had already been the governor since 2013, when he won 55 percent of the vote in a runoff and became the first elected official in the EU with an openly neo-Nazi past. He lost that regional seat after a surprise defeat in the fall 2017 elections.[15] Following the 2013 election, Moshe Kantor of the European Jewish Congress issued a statement urging action. "The neo-Nazis are gaining many political victories and are using the democratic system against democrats. Democracy has to fight back and European officials should immediately create a plan of action, including the proscription of neo-Nazi political parties, to deal with this phenomenon before it is too late," he said. "We hope the Greek model of suspending state funding for the Golden Dawn party and the revocation of parliamentary immunity for its members will be enacted elsewhere in Europe and form the basis of the opposition." Yet no such plan of action was drafted or put into place.

Chalking up the rise of the LSNS to an abandonment of class politics, the Slovakia-based Ervína Szabová Collective explained that the authoritarianism, corruption, and anti-Western rhetoric that pervaded decades of mainstream political conversations has created a fertile landscape for the far right. "The [LSNS] party's agitation—previously directed almost exclusively against 'Gypsy parasites'—was ... broadened to include bankers, politicians, and multinationals," the collective wrote in an October 2016 *Jacobin* article. "By tapping into feelings of social exclusion felt by poor Slovaks, including those who themselves have been compelled to migrate in search of work, Kotleba became one of the few figures in the Slovak political scene to address class politics."

On a snowy day in Banská Bystrica, Stanislav Mičev, the director of the Slovak National Uprising Museum, walked through the hallway and into a conference room decorated with paintings of Partisan guerilla fighters. Fastened on the far wall were rifles, ammunition belts, and army helmets used during that rebellion.

Mičev, who planned to challenge Kotleba for the regional governor's office later that year, took a seat and clasped his hands atop the oblong meeting table. In a sentence, he summed up the LSNS as "anti-Semitic, antiblack, anti-European, and antidemocratic."

A historian by trade, he explained that democrats, communist partisans, and other anti-fascist fighters launched the Slovak National Uprising in 1944 to fight back against the regime and its German allies. At its height, the number of anti-fascist fighters swelled to an estimated sixty thousand.

Although Tiso fled the country after the Soviet army occupied it in April 1945, he was later arrested in Bavaria and extradited to what had become communist Czechoslovakia. Two years later, he was taken to the gallows in Bratislava and hanged. For the

LSNS, Mičev explained, the uprising was a supposed plot against the country's first independent republic and a communist conspiracy against Slovakia's sovereignty.

While LSNS party members had toned down their rhetoric as they moved toward joining the mainstream political scene in recent years, the party had not abandoned its roots. "[Kotleba] used to wear the uniform similar to the [Nazi satellite state's] soldiers," Mičev stressed. "He adjusted the program to appear like it's committed to democratic principles. He doesn't express radical opinions as openly as before."

Yet he warned: "They put away those black uniforms and put on green shirts, but those uniforms are still sitting in storage somewhere."

Asked how the LSNS grew in popularity so rapidly, Mičev pointed to widespread discontent with the government's corruption and economic deprivation gripping large swaths of the rural population. Indeed, the LSNS grew in curious places, such as Kľak and Ostrý Grúň, two villages that were subjected to punitive attacks and razed by the First Slovak Republic's armed forces and its German allies.

Miroslav Seget, deputy mayor of the 589-person Ostrý Grúň village, explained that his own grandparents were evicted from their homes and displaced when the village was flattened in January 1945 as punishment for helping the anti-Nazi partisans.

Despite the massacre of some 145 villagers in Ostrý Grúň and Kľak, nearly one in five local voters cast their ballot for the LSNS last year. "My mother was born as the child of refugees," Seget said, shaking his head ominously. "It's a paradox because our village was burned down by the fascists [celebrated by the LSNS]. Kotleba got the second largest share of the vote in [Ostrý Grúň]." He opined: "We are partly responsible for Kotleba's support because we were neglecting young people."

Seget said he believed the phenomenon could be partially explained by the surviving generation's hesitance to speak openly about the massacre. "The memory of what happened in World War II is still present in the minds of the older generation, but that knowledge was not passed on because most of the survivors lost family members . . . and it's hard for them to talk about this period."

To combat the growth of the LSNS, Seget and others hope to better inform local youth about their heritage. On January 21, 2018, they held a public event in which survivors spoke to young people about their experience during the Second World War.

RIGHT-WING EXTREMISM

While liberal centrists view the rise of right-wing and far-right groups as an isolated phenomenon, the increasingly jingoistic and anti-immigrant rhetoric of the political mainstream paved the way for their ascendancy, often introducing the racist rhetoric that characterizes the LSNS and other groups on the far right.

Slovak prime minister Robert Fico was no exception. Direction–Social Democracy (SMER-SD), Fico's party, has been at the forefront of demonizing refugees and migrants as well as employing racist rhetoric about Roma, the ethnic minority that makes up around 10 percent of the country's total population.

In November 2015, following a string of ISIL-claimed terrorist attacks in Europe, Fico proudly declared that his country's security apparatus had been surveilling Muslim refugees, falsely equating them with far-right extremists. "We are monitoring every Muslim in our territory," Fico said outside the French embassy in Bratislava.[16] "We have increased monitoring of a refugee camp and detainment camps, as well as monitoring of far-right extremists."

Just a month earlier, he claimed Muslim refugees wouldn't like to live in Slovakia because of the absences of any mosques in the country. "We don't have any mosques in Slovakia so how can Muslims be integrated if they are not going to like it here?"

During the country's elections and afterward, Fico employed anti-immigrant and anti-Muslim rhetoric to mobilize nativist and populist sentiment. Throughout his campaign, Fico railed against refugees and migrants and promised not to honor the EU's refugee resettlement quota program.[17] The threat was largely nonexistent; only 330 asylum seekers had registered in the country the year before. In 2016, a mere sixteen people—eleven children and five mothers who came from Greek refugee camps—were relocated to Slovakia.[18]

Fico promised to protect "our women" from Muslims and decried the supposed intent of newcomers to create a "compact, closed Muslim community" in Slovakia, a possibility he said would be "a huge threat to the European way of life."

Lucia Najšlová, the Slovak editor in chief of regional current affairs website *V4 Revue*, summed up the impact of the prime minister's strategy in an interview with *Deutsche Welle* at the time: "He has contributed to an atmosphere of fear in Slovakia by framing migration as a threat."

Although the country is home to an almost invisible minority of Muslims, Fico declared in May 2016 that "Islam has no place" in Slovakia.[19] He went on to accuse refugees and migrants of "changing the face of the country."

Slovak foreign minister Miroslav Lajčák quickly joined the chorus of hate. In July 2016, he told *Deutsche Welle*: "Our people have not been exposed to Muslims and they are frightened. It's a new phenomenon for them.... Hundreds of Muslims mean nothing in Belgium or London, but it does mean something in Slovakia."

Later that year, in September, Fico announced his opposition to the distribution of refugees and migrants based on quotas.[20] "Quotas today clearly divide the EU, therefore I think they are politically finished," he said in Hungary ahead of that country's referendum on refugee quotas. "Whoever wants to divide Europe, let them put quotas on the table, who wants to unite Europe, let them come up with a different concept of fight[ing] against illegal migration."

Fico also used derogatory language when speaking of Roma, referring to them as "gypsies" and accusing them in February 2017 of "abusing" the welfare system. The leader's frequent use of racist and xenophobic language only served to legitimize the rhetoric of the LSNS and its ideological allies—and it did so at a time when extremism was soaring among the ranks of the far right.

Fico's comments were not mere slipups. In what the Hate Speech International watchdog group described as an obvious attempt to "win back former [SMER] voters" from the far right, the ruling party created a coalition with the ultraconservative Sieť party, the Hungarian-Slovak Most–Híd party, and the Slovak National Party, a far-right outfit with a history of anti-Hungarian xenophobia.[21] In light of this, it is not surprising that few people were convinced in May 2017 when Fico appealed for law enforcement to intervene and shut down the proliferation of far-right ideas by the LSNS and other like-minded parties and movements.[22]

An April 2017 report by the Political Capital Policy Research and Consulting Institute warned of violent radicalization of far-right and neo-Nazi groups that were engaging in paramilitary training and cultivating ties with the Russian Federation's ruling wing. The report described LSNS patrols as part of an orchestrated effort to establishment paramilitary-like forces. As far back as December 2012, Kotleba had sought to register a civil society organization that functioned as an LSNS-led militia. First called Guards of the LSNS, he later changed the name to Guards of the People. Although the application was rejected, the report said the effort was "symbolic of the organization's intentions."

It did not stop there. In October 2016, the Slovak parliament outlawed vigilante patrols by LSNS members that targeted Roma passengers on trains. Donning the party's signature green shirts, the vigilantes would board trains and intimidate Roma, often hurling racist slurs and threats. Activists and watchdogs accused the LSNS of continuing the vigilante patrols nonetheless.

RUSSIAN TIES

The LSNS, however, was not the sole actor on the far-right political stage. Although many groups share its apparent vision of a white ethno-state, some disagree with what they consider to be Kotleba's pandering to the mainstream political establishment and supposed betrayal of the struggle by entering the parliamentary process.

Another prominent far-right group is the Slovak Revival Movement, a political movement that also praises the legacy of Jozef Tiso and the First Slovak Republic, often justifying its deportation of Jews during the Second World War.[23] The group's Slovak-language website is littered with anti-Semitic content and expressions of solidarity with Russia's deadly intervention in the Syrian Civil War.

The relationship went far beyond proclamations of solidarity, however. The Slovak Revival Movement also boasts of its partnership with the Dobrovolec (Volunteer), a Russian ultranationalist club that has played a key role in recruiting volunteers to deploy with pro-Putin militias in Donbass, the region of Ukraine occupied by Russia.

The group's involvement in pro-Russian paramilitary formations was not uncommon among Slovakia's far-right organizations. The Slovak Conscripts (SB), a pan-Slavic, pro-Russian paramilitary group, models its vision for the future on the far-right Putin regime. It brags of providing military training to children in its seventeen territorial units consisting of approximately 150 members. These units engaged in training for "outdoor survival, first aid, hygiene, and military tactics (both conventional and guerrilla fighting style), also the handling of weapons, the close combat, topography, radiation, chemical, and biological protection."

Although the SB distanced itself from the open admiration of wartime Nazism and commemorates the communist forces that liberated the country from its fascist regime, the group calls for pan-Slavic solidarity and advocates a Slovak ethno-state with close ties or incorporation into the Russian Federation. A former member of the organization, Martin Keptra, openly proclaimed that he joined pro-Russian militiamen in Ukraine to fight for "Slavic interests, values, traditions, family—something that allegedly the EU represses and fundamentally denies."

Action Group Resistance Kysuce, a neo-Nazi paramilitary outfit headed by Marián Magát, was founded in 2010 as one of the more hardline groups on the far right. It engaged in extreme anti-Semitism and often slyly expresses support for the Holocaust.

FIGHTING BACK: ANTI-FASCISTS IN THE STREETS

Around noon on March 13, more than a thousand anti-fascists assembled in central Bratislava for a counterprotest. But their hopes of meeting LSNS and other far-right demonstrators in the streets were dashed when that protest was canceled.

A large white tarp spanned the lawn in front of a Slovak National Uprising monument. Printed on it was a swastika, a thick red circle and diagonal line painted over it, signifying "No!" Slovaks, Czechs, and Hungarians who came in solidarity stood on the gray grass, listening. A group of teenagers in denim and leather jackets sat on a nearby ledge, puffing cigarettes and passing around a bottle of beer.

The speeches came to an end, and the Antifa protesters set off. They marched in columns through the city, chanting against Kotleba's party. "Alerta, alerta, anti-fascista," they sang out. "Say it loud and say it clear, refugees are welcome here," they cried in English.

A host of flags and banners bobbed above the marchers. "Always Antifa," a green and orange flag read. "Goodnight white pride" had been scrawled on a black banner under a hand-painted Czech Antifa logo and a stick figure kicking a swastika.

The protesters moved from the main roads and weaved into the historic old city's arteries and alleyways. The sound of their footsteps reverberated through the corridors. Police officers walked along and observed, occasionally muttering directives into walkie-talkies. The march eventually arrived in a square and morphed into a drum session, with protesters still singing anti-fascist chants in unison.

Twenty-nine-year-old Matúš Budovic held up a sign and sang

along. He had traveled more than two hundred miles from his village, Ráztočno, to "set an example" for the country's youth by standing up to the LSNS. As he spoke, wisps of cigarette smoke rose from the crowd beyond him, twirling and dragging against the dimming afternoon sun. "We've seen this situation before. When the neo-Nazis are on the rise, they attack [minorities] and Antifa activists," Budovic said, adding that far-right provocateurs attacked him at an anti-fascist rally ten years ago. "History can repeat itself because their generation has grown up, but there is a new one now."

While not huge in numbers, anti-fascists in Slovakia have enjoyed a tradition of shutting down far-right rallies and confronting the LSNS and others in the streets. In 2015, as LSNS supporters gathered in the capital to commemorate the Nazi-era regime, an anti-fascist blockade prevented around 150 neo-Nazis from successfully marching on a planned route.[24] "Those who subscribe to the legacy of the Independent Slovak State even today argue that it provided a good life for its inhabitants, but they deny the fact that murder and violence have nothing in common with a good life or with respectability," Nazi-Free Bratislava said of the direct action in a statement.

A year earlier, Together Against Fascism, an anti-fascist initiative, prevented neo-Nazis from gathering for their annual commemoration to remember the Tiso regime. Between 150 and three hundred people, according to media reports, came out to oppose the LSNS and their far-right allies.[25] "Today's march is a

clear 'no' to fascism in all of its forms. It publicly rejects nationalism, neo-Nazism, anti-Semitism and, on the contrary, voices
the message of a tolerant and inclusive society," organizer Robert Mihály told local media at the rally.

SPREADING EXTREMIST PROPAGANDA AND
SHUTTING DOWN ANTIRACIST CRITIQUES

With Fico and the mainstream political elite legitimizing the antirefugee discourse, the LSNS party has been able to push a more
extreme version of the rhetoric, particularly in social media. In
June 2017, a Facebook post, which was published by a user who
was a fan of the LSNS page and had a timeline full of antirefugee
and racist comments, claimed that migrants were paid a monthly
stipend of one thousand euros, while Slovaks were left with only
four hundred euros a month. The post claimed that refugees and
migrants were also provided free accommodation and food. It received more than fourteen hundred likes and was shared widely.
The *Slovak Spectator*, however, exposed the claims as a hoax: Slovakia's minimum wage is 435 euros a month, and refugees and
migrants do not receive such a stipend from the Slovak government.[26]

Meanwhile, a month earlier, the LSNS filed a criminal complaint over a play titled *Natálka*, which told the true story of far-
right extremists attacking and gravely injuring a Roma family
with Molotov cocktails in the neighboring Czech Republic in 2009.

As a result of the actual incident, a two-year-old Roma girl was left with 80 percent of her body burned. In the complaint, LSNS legislators claimed the play qualified as defamation of nation, race, and beliefs, citing a scene in which a neo-Nazi scribbles a swastika and fascist slogans on a wall.[27] The police later dismissed the complaint.

Spreading "fake news"—the term popularized in 2016 by the mainstream U.S. media and bastardized by far-right U.S. president Donald Trump—has been a key strategy of Kotleba and his followers. In March 2017, a Slovak tabloid published a blog post claiming that the United States was planning to build a secret base in Slovakia. It claimed that Kotleba and a far-right paramilitary group could protect the country from U.S. occupation.[28] The problem, though, was that the plans didn't exist.

Kotleba, who was deemed "Homophobe of the Year" in 2016 by local rights groups, also organized an anti-LGBTQI rally as a counterprotest to the annual gay pride march. Exploiting widespread homophobia, the LSNS used the event, which had not received a permit, to obtain signatures for petitions calling on Slovakia to leave NATO and the EU.[29] Two thousand marchers pushed back nonetheless and rallied in the Old City, demanding LGBTQI rights in a country where religious conservatism has been one of the main obstacles to social progress.

In May 2017, the LSNS claimed it had obtained half of the requisite 350,000 signatures on a petition demanding that the country withdraw from NATO. Local media cast doubts on the claim, explaining that a petition falls short of the referendum necessary to bind the government to such a decision.[30] The lie was republished by a Russian news site that inaccurately stated Slovakia would withdraw from the alliance by 2020.

While there are worthy arguments that can be made for distrusting NATO and the EU and for leaving those entities, the LSNS, like Trump in the United States, has exploited nativist and protectionist sentiments to advance a far-right agenda.

THE POETRY OF FASCISM

On the damp morning of March 14, LSNS members were visiting poor families in need of financial assistance.[31] They distributed three checks—each of which was for 1,488 euros. Photos of the visit were posted on Facebook, and the party was later accused of—and investigated for—choosing those numbers intentionally with a nod and a wink. Fourteen, it was said, refers to the white supremacist slogan "14 words," while 88 referred to the Nazi greeting "Heil Hitler"—with eight representing the eighth letter of the alphabet, H.

Elsewhere that same day, sleet covered the dead grass outside a modest lavender home in the northern village of Oščadnica like bits of confetti. The piercing wind picked up, keeping afloat a host of identical LSNS flags, green cloth dancing under the murky winter sky.

Within the thirty-person crowd, greetings all around. "At guard," they said to one another, saluting coyly, using a fascist phrase that was popular under Tiso's rule. The green-clad audience formed rows and stood with folded hands over their laps, as local LSNS official František Drozd placed a multicolored wreath of flowers at the foot of the home where Tiso once lived. Drozd broke the momentary silence and welcomed the crowd. As the Sunday morning mass concluded across the street, church-goers poured out of the church. A handful of them—dressed smartly in church digs—joined the procession.

A gaggle of police officers stood next to their cars in the adjacent parking lot, rubbing their gloved hands together to stay warm, boredom sketched across their faces.

A short, husky bald man, Drozd launched into an angry tirade. He railed against those the LSNS has designated as Slovakia's enemies: refugees and migrants, Muslims and Roma, NATO and the United States, Israel, and the European Union.

Without a microphone in hand, he blasted through a laundry list of Slovakia's ailments: a faltering economy, corruption, a perceived loss of sovereignty, and supposed threats to its overwhelmingly white demographic terrain. "How would our first president, Jozef Tiso, see Slovakia today?" he implored with a nod of righteousness.

"What would Tiso think if he saw retired Slovaks struggling to survive on dwindling pensions?" Drozd asked the lot. "The European Union, with its insane laws, only does harm to Slovakia," he said. "Migrants, who have been invited by the EU, are coming to Europe in the thousands."

Apparently irrelevant was the tiny number of refugees and

migrants—a mere 146 in 2016, most of whom were Ukrainian and not from Muslim-majority countries—who sought safety in Slovakia, a country relatively untouched by the crisis that saw hundreds of thousands of people flee war and economic devastation to reach Europe. For Drozd and the LSNS, the numbers were a mere distraction. Theirs is a politics of redemption, of reviving the short-lived motherland of the First Slovak Republic.

Here Drozd switched to a poem, an ode to Kotleba and the party's vision for Slovakia. "Marian Kotleba has planted a small seed / And it grew into a big, beautiful tree / It has a treetop with branches and is blossoming and blossoming / There will be a rich harvest for those who desire the fruit."

Andrej Medvecký, another LSNS member, took Drozd's place on the soapbox. "Many of you here experienced communism, and the regime today is even worse," he started.

"People are going to prison for their opinions," Medvecký lamented, referring to Sheila Szmerekova, a twenty-four-year-old Slovak facing legal retribution for broadcasting online a video of herself urinating on a Qur'an before setting it ablaze. In that low-quality cellphone video, she squats on the Muslim holy book, soiling its torn pages as a Slovak flag hangs behind her.

She launched into a tirade in the video: "I will hunt you [Muslims] all one by one. No matter if it is a woman, child, or man. I will bump off anybody who gets in my way."

Medvecký orated, and those in the crowd shook their heads in collective indignation. He said: "If we think about March 14 [the anniversary of the First Slovak Republic's establishment], some agree [about its significance] and others don't. Those who don't agree are not true Slovaks."

As the speeches concluded and the commemoration came to an end, a dull crescendo of applause floated upward from the audience. The mass broke apart and they snapped selfies before assembling again for a round of group photos. Snap, snap, snap—the cameras captured the final moments. In every frame, the green flags waved proudly above them.

NEW WEAPONS

Citing violent rhetoric, Alena Krempaská, program director at the Bratislava-based Human Rights Institute, placed a portion of the blame on the LSNS for attacks targeting Roma, Muslims, and LGBTQ people in recent years. "They incite violence and hatred and a general atmosphere of hatred against Roma, Muslims and LGBTQ people," she said, sitting on a couch in the institute's office. "While the majority of people are disillusioned with the mainstream parties and there is no alternative on the left, they [the LSNS] were gaining support."

Arguing that the mainstream media and political establishment have facilitated the growth of the LSNS and other far-right outlets by adopting similar anti-immigrant discourse, Krempaská said: "Now they're seen as a serious political force, but they were a fringe group, nothing, a few years ago."

When asked how to push back against their growing strength, she said people in impoverished parts of the country, especially youth, needed hope for a better future. And only one party, the LSNS, has promised to speak to their needs. "They seem to have voted for Kotleba not because he's a fascist but despite it."

For that fight, Krempaská said effective organization and strategic planning were keys. "The old-school idea of Antifa—justice in the streets and direct confrontation—is less effective in these circumstances." Instead, she explained, "We must use different types of weapons and make different kinds of alliances." Otherwise, she feared, the LSNS would continue to swell its ranks.

Rado Sloboda, a twenty-six-year-old activist in Banská Bystrica, was one of several organizers who worked on the Not in Our Town campaign. Sitting in a noisy café in Bratislava before the anti-fascist protest on March 13, he explained that they sought to educate young people about human rights and the danger of right-wing extremism. Sloboda said they had recently launched a pilot version of an educational program in primary and secondary schools. They bring people from marginalized groups—Jews, Muslims, Roma, and refugees, among others—to speak to the students.

As the LSNS has targeted young people by creating youth leagues and other political and social organizations, Sloboda and his colleagues hoped to offer an alternative. They recruited more than twenty core members and one hundred volunteers.

Indeed, youth appeared to be the largest base of Kotleba's support. According to a December 2016 study by the Institute for

Public Affairs, around one-third of young people sympathized with the LSNS party's activities, while some 30 percent supported Kotleba himself—a far higher proportion than the national average.[32]

"We used to believe that they [LSNS] mainly spread among young boys from poor families," Sloboda said, explaining that Kotleba and his followers regularly accused Sloboda's group of being "foreign agents."

"From time to time, we have direct actions and public events and they ask about who finances this," Sloboda continued. He worried that if the number of Kotleba's followers continued to grow, the LSNS would be empowered. Although Kotleba lost his regional seat in Banská Bystrica in late 2017, the party still had fourteen seats in the parliament. "There will be more mobilization on both sides." The breakneck pace of the party's growth was "really troubling for the future," he concluded. "It can really get much more radical and much more violent."

Later that month, hundreds of Slovaks gathered outside the LSNS party headquarters in Banská Bystrica to protest. Among those who addressed the crowd were Holocaust survivors, prominent athletes, politicians, and Ján Benčík. "Even if they put in the name of their party that this Slovakia is theirs, in reality it belongs to all of us," Benčík said to the crowd. "But Slovakia is not yours, make no mistake, we are not leaving it to you."

NOTES

1. Patrick Strickland, "Fighting Slovakia's Far Right Online and on the Streets," *Al Jazeera English*, June 13, 2017, http://www.aljazeera.com/indepth/features/2017/05/fighting-slovakia-online-streets-170529083248638.html.

2. "Slovakia: Thousands Protest Kotleba and Clerical Fascism in Bratislava," *Romea.cz*, March 7, 2016, http://www.romea.cz/en/news/world/slovakia-thousands-protest-kotleba-and-clerical-fascism-in-bratislava.

3. Peter Dlhopolec, "Extremists Thrive on Facebook, despite Recent Shutdowns," *Slovak Spectator*, May 17, 2017, https://spectator.sme.sk/c/20534719/extremists-thrive-on-facebook-despite-recent-shut-downs.html.

4. Lucia Krbatova, "University Students Support Extremists too, Some Want out of the EU," *Slovak Spectator*, May 10, 2017, https://spectator.sme.sk/c/20529291/university-students-support-extremists-too-some-want-out-of-the-eu.html.

5. "New Far Rightist Legislator Arrives at Slovak Parliament with Firearm," *Xinhua*, March 22, 2016, http://news.xinhuanet.com/english/2016-03/22/c_135210205.htm.

6. "Police Confiscate Firearms and Gun Permit of ĽSNS MP," *Slovak Spectator*, March 30, 2016, https://spectator.sme.sk/c/20127445/police-confiscate-firearms-and-gun-permit-of-lsns-mp.html.

7. "Slovak Neo-Nazi MP, Milan Mazurek, Caught on Camera Attacking Muslims in Slovakia," *TellMAMA*, March 14, 2016, https://tellmamauk.org/slovak-neo-nazi-mp/.

8. "Mazurek Not Prosecuted for Holocaust Denial," *Slovak Spectator*, September 7, 2016, https://spectator.sme.sk/c/20266405/mazurek-not-prosecuted-for-holocaust-denial.html.

9 "ĽSNS MPs Got Highest Fine for Statements on Islam," *Slovak Spectator*, February 9, 2017, https://spectator.sme.sk/c/20455244/lsns-mps-got-highest-fine-for-statements-on-islam.html.

10. "Slovak Neo-Nazi and MP Milan Mazurek Prosecuted for Racist Re-

marks about Roma," *Romea.cz*, March 21, 2017, http://www.romea.cz/en/news/world/slovak-neo-nazi-and-mp-milan-mazurek-prosecuted-for-racist-remarks-about-roma.

11. Aaron Lake Smith, "The New Roma Ghettoes," *Vice*, December 25, 2013, https://www.vice.com/en_us/article/wdpmdm/the-new-roma-ghettos-000519-v20n4.

12. Ishaan Thahoor, "Before They Opposed Muslims, Europe's Far Right Targeted a Different Minority," *Washington Post*, June 22, 2016, https://www.washingtonpost.com/news/worldviews/wp/2016/06/22/before-they-opposed-muslims-europes-far-right-targeted-a-different-minority.

13. Beata Balogová, "Hurbanovo Shooting Sparks Fears," *Slovak Spectator*, June 27, 2012, https://spectator.sme.sk/c/20043872/hurbanovo-shooting-sparks-fears.html.

14. The Ervina Szabova Collective, "Slovakia Needs an Alternative," *Jacobin*, April 20, 2016, https://www.jacobinmag.com/2016/04/slovakia-marian-kotleba-roma-lsns-immigration-orban/.

15. Tatiana Jancarikova, "Slovakia's Far-Right Party, Ruling Leftists Lose Regional Elections," Reuters, November 5, 2017, https://www.reuters.com/article/us-slovakia-election-extremists/slovakias-far-right-party-ruling-leftists-lose-regional-elections-idUSKBN1D501P.

16. Rose Troup Buchanan, "'We Are Monitoring Every Muslim' after Paris Attacks, Claims Slovakian PM," *Independent*, November 17, 2015, http://www.independent.co.uk/news/world/europe/we-are-monitoring-every-muslim-after-paris-attacks-claims-slovakian-pm-a6737851.html.

17. Ian Willoughby, "Slovak PM Set for Election Win with Anti-migrant Rhetoric," *Deutsche Welle*, April 3, 2016, http://www.dw.com/en/slovak-pm-set-for-election-win-with-anti-migrant-rhetoric/a-19089588.

18. Roman Cuprik, "Asylum Seekers Avoid Slovakia," *Slovak Spectator*, July 11, 2017, https://spectator.sme.sk/c/20579285/asylum-seekers-avoid-slovakia.html.

19. Vince Chadwick, "Robert Fico: 'Islam Has No Place in Slovakia,'" *Po-*

litico, May 27, 2016, http://www.politico.eu/article/robert-fico-islam-no-place-news-slovakia-muslim-refugee/.

20. Josh Lowe, "Slovakia's Prime Minister Says Refugee Relocation Quotas Are 'Finished,'" *Newsweek*, October 3, 2016, http://www.newsweek.com/eu-refugees-robert-fico-viktor-orban-quotas-refugee-crisis-relocation-503601.

21. "The Kotleba Phenomenon," Hate Speech International, January 3, 2017, https://www.hate-speech.org/kotleba-phenomenon.

22. "Fico: Police Should Intervene against Extremists," *Slovak Spectator*, May 10, 2017, https://spectator.sme.sk/c/20529313/fico-police-should-inter vene-against-extremists.html.

23. Radovan Bránik and Grigorij Mesežnikov, "Hatred, Violence and Com-prehensive Military Training," Political Capital Research and Consulting Insti-tute, 2017, http://www.politicalcapital.hu/pc-admin/source/documents/PC_NED_country_study_SK_20170428.pdf.

24. "Slovakia: Antifascists Try to Block Neo-Nazi March Celebrating WWII-Era Fascist State," *Romea.cz*, March 14, 2015, http://www.romea.cz/en/news/slovakia-antifascists-try-to-block-neo-nazi-march-celebrating-wwii-era-fas cist-state.

25. Michaela Terenzani, "Anti-fascist Protest Takes Place in Bratislava," *Slovak Spectator*, March 23, 2014, https://spectator.sme.sk/c/20050178/anti-fascist-protest-takes-place-in-bratislava.html.

26. "Do Migrants Earn Hundreds of Euros More than Slovaks for the Same Jobs?," *Slovak Spectator*, June 26, 2017, https://spectator.sme.sk/c/20568836/do-migrants-earn-hundreds-of-euros-more-than-slovaks-for-the-same-jobs .html.

27. "Police Turns Down Complaint against Natálka Play," *Slovak Spectator*, May 9, 2017, https://spectator.sme.sk/c/20528244/police-turns-down-compl aint-against-natalka-play.html.

28. "American Military Base in Slovakia and War in Europe Are Hoaxes," *Slovak Spectator*, March 17, 2017, https://spectator.sme.sk/c/20485867/amer ican-military-base-in-slovakia-and-war-in-europe-are-hoaxes.html.

29. Radia Minarechová, "Pride Back in Bratislava," *Slovak Spectator*, August 8, 2016, https://spectator.sme.sk/c/20232117/pride-back-in-bratislava.html.

30. "Slovakia to Leave NATO Is a Hoax," *Slovak Spectator*, May 29, 2017, https://spectator.sme.sk/c/20542136/slovakia-to-leave-nato-is-a-hoax.html.

31. "Kotleba's Far-Right Party Faces Prosecution for '1488' Donation," *Slovak Spectator*, May 4, 2017, https://spectator.sme.sk/c/20524510/kotlebas-far-right-party-faces-prosecution-for-1488-donation.html.

32. "Slovakia: Many Youth Support the Ultra-right, Study Finds," *Romea.cz*, December 12, 2016 http://www.romea.cz/en/news/world/slovakia-many-youth-support-the-ultra-right-study-finds.

ITALY

On the outskirts of Rome sits Quarticciolo, a working-class neighborhood ravaged by neoliberal-induced poverty, institutional deprivation, home evictions, and drug trafficking. Fabrizio Troya, a twenty-year-old university student and lifelong Quarticciolo resident, wore a black, tightly fitted Adidas jumpsuit on a brisk evening in January 2018. He stood across the room from a boxing ring situated in the corner. On the walls, photos of famous boxers like Mike Tyson and Quarticciolo's local athletes hung next to images of protesters clashing with police and anti-fascist propaganda posters.

Troya was one of the founding members of Palestra Popolare Quarticciolo, an anti-fascist gym in a building occupied by local autonomous and left-wing activists who had been part of the Red Lab collective years earlier. "I was born and raised here," Troya said. "My grandmother came here when Mussolini evicted them from the center of Rome."

The entire neighborhood chipped in to help build the gym after the activists took over the abandoned building. "This gym is for the neighborhood, by the neighborhood," Troya explained, recalling local residents participating in everything from constructing and renovating the space to bringing food and coffee. "Residents saw it as a miracle because state institutions are completely absent here," he said, explaining that Quarticciolo has been plagued by a lack of resources and projects from the Italian government.

With the far right gaining ground in a number of adjacent neighborhoods and areas, Palestra Popolare Quarticciolo served as one of many community-initiated projects that highlighted the efforts of anti-fascists to contribute to the improvement of their local community. Down the road, a large apartment block has also been occupied by local activists to resist the evictions of poor families and working-class locals from their homes in the crisis-hit economy.

The gym was designed with the hope of providing an alternative to both organized crime, which targeted teenagers and youngsters to sell drugs, and the growing allure of the far right among many Italians. "This place is about teaching good values, sports, and anti-fascism," he explained. "This is the alternative."

"This neighborhood reflects Italian society at the moment. Here you see all the difficulties," Troya said. "The fascists tried to come here once for political purposes—we rejected them easily, and they never came back."

Troya argued that the activities of anti-fascists here and elsewhere defy the widespread depictions of the movement as young men looking for fights. Although he himself was arrested two years earlier over a fight with a fascist activist, he explained that education, monitoring the far right, and community projects are the backbone of the movement. "This is long-term work, but it gives you satisfaction. At first, we had nothing. Now we have a hundred kids coming to this place every day, looking for somewhere to get off the streets." He added: "It's beautiful to beat a fascist, but it's much more beautiful to help a kid find a way off the streets."

The volunteers at Popolare Palestra Quarticciolo had made a habit of patrolling adjacent neighborhoods to rip fascist propaganda off the walls. "We don't speak with the fascists," he added, disputing the stale argument that the best way of defeating the far right is to debate them in the realm of ideas. "There is nothing to say to the fascists."

Stressing the importance of educational initiatives as a central keystone of anti-fascist activism, he said: "People are tired of the mainstream politicians, and racism is bred by ignorance."

GROWTH OF THE FAR RIGHT

In the leadup to the March 2018 national elections, Italy was gripped by fear over the growth of neofascist parties, such as CasaPound and Forza Nuova. In November 2017, CasaPound had landed a seat on the Ostia district council in a suburb of Rome, exacerbating the worries harbored by anti-fascists and antiracists.

When I met anti-fascist activist Diego Gianella in Ostia, he said that he had been attacked by members of the CasaPound fascist party six times.[1] On a wintry day in early January 2018, the twenty-seven-year-old escaped the piercing wind and ducked into a timeworn bar outside a train station in Ostia, the crisis-hit coastal suburb of Rome where he lives.

Removing his jacket, he quickly ordered a coffee and stood at the bar. Gianella, a charismatic man with a patchy beard, spoke with jubilance despite running through a laundry list of violence he attributed to CasaPound, which made historic inroads in municipal elections the previous November, obtaining 9 percent of the overall vote. He said CasaPound supporters have slashed his tires five times, bashed his car windows four times, tagged graffiti on his sedan twice, and vandalized his home once.

While CasaPound members in the poverty-stricken suburb of Italy's capital have denied such allegiations, Gianella was one of several local anti-fascist activists and critics of the self-proclaimed fascist party who have accused its supporters of targeting them with violence.

The pompoms dangling from the braided strings of his black-and-gray beanie shook along with his head as he recalled one of the most egregious assaults, which took place one morning in February 2017. On that day, Gianella was rushing to a city council meeting—"running late as usual," he says—when he spotted CasaPound members posted next to the entrance.

Known in Ostia for his outspoken anti-fascism, he opted to enter the building from the rear entrance rather than risk a confrontation. Yet, he hadn't gone unnoticed. When a guard informed him that he could only enter the building from the main entrance out front, he decided to make his way home instead, so he headed toward the parking lot. Waiting at his car, however, was a gang of five CasaPound supporters, he recalled. Recognizing one of the young men as a former classmate, Gianella asked what they were doing at his car. "Then he hit me, and I fell," he remembered. Within seconds of hitting the pavement, a salvo of kicks and punches thudded against Gianella's flanks as he put his hands up to protect his head. His attackers left him on the ground with busted lips, a mouth full of blood, and three broken ribs. "Go tell the police now," they mocked him.

Born as a political movement in 2003, when far-rightists occupied a vacant municipal building in central Rome, CasaPound's name is an ode to the American poet Ezra Pound, a supporter of Italian fascist leader Benito Mussolini.

GROWING INFLUENCE

In November, CasaPound clinched around six thousand votes in Ostia's municipal elections—a nearly 600 percent increase from the previous elections just a few years earlier. CasaPound's newfound success in Ostia came on the heels of the party securing 9 percent of the votes in Lucca's mayoral elections in June and landing its members on city councils in nearby Todi and the northern city of Bolzano.

With CasaPound's Luca Marsella, a vocal fascist who had been accused of violent threats, now a district councillor in Ostia, the elections prompted fear among political opponents and analysts who worried about the return of fascism. Guido Caldiron, author of *Extreme Right*, a book that examines the growth of the far right in Europe and elsewhere, said the electoral results in Ostia were "very important because Rome is CasaPound's core. For them, it's a very significant victory."

Describing CasaPound as a "militarized entity" whose supporters carry out attacks while the party's brass denies any affiliation with bloodshed, Caldiron said: "Even when they are involved in violence, they always try to cover it." The efforts at protecting its brand and presenting a respectable face to the public, Caldiron argued, distinguished CasaPound from others that openly celebrate violence against anti-fascists and migrants. "They have people who are legitimate criminals, and they have to control that—it's a controlled form of neofascism," he explained. "You can be violent, but you have to accept certain rules and not show off about your violence. . . . It is all part of a package designed to maintain the façade of respectability."

And despite regularly denying complicity in violence, Casa-Pound's members and supporters have a lengthy history of attacks. In December 2011, a fifty-year-old CasaPound supporter in Florence shot dead two Senegalese street traders and injured three others before turning the gun on himself and committing suicide. CasaPound activist Alberto Palladino was sentenced to two years in prison for an attack that hospitalized five activists from the center-left Democratic Party that same year. The fascist party claimed that he was wrongfully convicted.

"IF THERE WERE NO ANTI-FASCISTS, THERE WOULD BE NO VIOLENCE"

On a chilly morning in early January, a self-described "militant" opened the door of CasaPound's squat in central Rome. Inside, he pointed to the walls of the corridor, colorfully painted with the names of the party's heroes. Italian leader Benito Mussolini and philosopher Friedrich Nietzsche, important historical inspirations for contemporary fascists, were among the more obvious names. Less explicable were names such as Ahmad Shah Massoud, the late Afghan militia leader who battled the Soviets and the Taliban alike, and Jack Kerouac, the American novelist and pioneer of the Beat Generation.

Simone Di Stefano, CasaPound's candidate for prime minister in the upcoming national elections in March, insisted that the party's gains in Ostia were an important development in an area "that has been abandoned by the state" and unfairly branded as a "mafia city." Swaddled in a black winter coat, Di Stefano ran his hand through his short, salt-and-pepper hair while sitting in the conference room. The walls were blanketed in party propaganda announcing conferences and celebrating visits by far-right parties from across Europe. One of the posters announced a 2014 meeting between CasaPound and party officials from Golden Dawn, the neofascist party in nearby Greece. On an adjacent wall sat a framed CasaPound poster brandishing the face of Julius Evola, the Italian philosopher whose work sought to advance fascism.

Since its establishment fourteen years earlier, CasaPound had opened 106 offices across the country and boasted of twenty thousand card-carrying members. In recent years, the party successfully broadened its base by taking aim at refugees and migrants, capitalizing on Euroscepticism, and squatting in buildings to protest Italy's housing crisis. While leftists and anarchists had for decades occupied buildings on behalf of people displaced by evictions and carried out social projects such as distributing food to the poor, CasaPound's cooptation of the tactics comes with an important distinction: Italians only.

Confronted with allegations of attacks, Di Stefano did not deny that CasaPound's supporters participated in physical confrontations: "If there were no anti-fascists, there would be no violence." Di Stefano pointed to an incident in January 2017 when a police officer was injured while attempting to diffuse an explosive device placed outside a CasaPound-linked bookstore in Florence. The fascist leader rejects Gianella's accusations as "lies," adding that CasaPound has attempted to sue the Ostia-based anti-fascist for libel. Di Stefano instead blamed the media and anti-fascists for violence, dubbing them agents of "globalism," a term that carries anti-Semitic undertones. "There is no actual evidence [of CasaPound] doing physical attacks," he claims. "The only attacks here have been done by anti-fascists."

"I WANTED TO SAY: 'FASCISM IS SHITTY' "

Back in Ostia, however, local leaders and residents dismissed Di Stefano's claims of innocence. Witnessing CasaPound gaining steam around him, Franco De Donno, a priest who has lived in Ostia since 1981, decided in the fall of 2017 to run in the municipal elections. Now a district councillor, he found himself sitting across the table from the fascist party's Marsella during municipal meetings. Explaining that he was born on June 2, 1946, the day that Italy became a republic, De Donno said: "Being democratic and anti-fascist is in my DNA."

Sitting in a café on Ostia's main square, De Donno recounted leaving the church in August 2017 to find a band of CasaPound members holding up a banner accusing him of being a traitor for his open support of refugees and migrants. While De Donno had not been targeted with physical harm, he pointed the finger at Ca-saPound for fostering a climate of violence. In response, the priest helped form a network of solidarity activists and social justice-minded members of the faith community. "If this mentality of exclusion [of migrants and others] continues, there will be no peace and no development," he argued, "but the strongest enemy that needs to be defeated is indifference [to fascism]."

Carlo, a sixteen-year-old Ostia local who asked that I use a pseudonym for him, alternated between brief drags from a cigarette and sips of an espresso outside a rundown café in central Ostia. His mohawk drooped to the left as he leaned forward, arguing that young people should get involved in anti-fascism early on. Carlo recalled a pair of assaults he says were carried out by CasaPound supporters who targeted him for his presence at anti-fascist rallies in the town square.

Finishing the espresso, he used a small spoon to scoop up and eat a soggy clump of sugar from the bottom of the coffee cup. His oversized leather jacket hung loosely on his lanky torso; his jeans crumpled at the bottom where they were tucked messily into his black military-style boots. During the summer of 2017, Carlo recalled, he was walking in central Ostia when a CasaPound supporter—an adult male—stopped him to ask if he had been present at anti-fascist demonstrations in front of the party's offices. "What?" he replied, surprised by the question. Then a fist crashed into his eye. "What the fuck? I didn't do anything," Carlo said.

Although Carlo initially went to the police, he subsequently decided not to press charges because he did not trust law enforcement, which has in the past been linked to the mob. And like many critics of CasaPound, the teenager believed the fascist party is similarly linked to the local mafia. "Then other people started threatening me," he explains. "They said, 'We'll shoot you.'" From that day on, when CasaPound supporters saw him in the street, he said, they hurled insults and threats in his direction. "They called me a 'shitty hippie' and a 'communist faggot.'"

A few months later, when Carlo and his girlfriend were passing time on a lazy evening in a pub, a group of seven CasaPound supporters—all of them adults—called him over to their table. "What do you think about fascism?" one of the men asked him. Fearing another attack, Carlo replied simply: "It's an important part of our country's history." He remembered: "I wanted to say, 'Fascism is shitty,' but I couldn't." After a brief exchange, the man grabbed Carlo by the collar, pulled him close, and threatened him. When Carlo broke free, a fist narrowly missed his face. One of the men yelled at him and his girlfriend: "You deserve to have cocks on your face."

Worried by the prospect of yet more violence, Carlo had to change his daily routine, taking alternate routes through his neighborhood, mapped carefully to avoid CasaPound's office and hangouts frequented by the party's supporters. Nonetheless, Carlo insisted that he would continue to protest against Casa-Pound and other far-right groups. "I'm not scared [to protest]. Everyone fears being beaten up, but I can get over that because I believe in the [anti-fascist] cause and have my ideals," he said. "I will keep standing on the front line because I must do so."

On a pale January afternoon in 2018, seventeen-year-old Ali sat around a fading fire at Baobab Experience, a makeshift refugee transit center situated in a bedraggled parking lot next to deserted buildings on the outskirts of Rome.[2] When Ali decided to make the journey to Europe and left Khartoum, the Sudanese capital, he was just fifteen years old. His hopes to study and find work, however, were put on hold when he was trapped in Libya for two years. With the sun slumping beyond the horizon, Ali recalled finally arriving on Italy's southern shores a month ago. "We've tried to cross the border already [into France]," he told me. "They returned us to southern Italy, and we came all the way back here."

Baobab Experience, which was established in 2015, had to move from location to location because of a slate of evictions—twenty as of January 2018. "We don't want to stay in Italy," Ali said. "Even people with [legal] papers here end up sleeping in the streets with us." Although few refugees and migrants sought to remain in Italy, where job opportunities were scarce, the far right had seized on increasing frustration among many Italians to push a nativist and antimigrant program.

While Guido Caldiron acknowledged that CasaPound and Forza Nuova had slim chances of breaking the 3 percent threshold to enter parliament in the March 2018 elections, he argued that their antimigrant crusades may improve their chances in future local and regional elections. "They exploit the crisis to get consensus in certain areas by leading revolts against the presence of immigrants," he said, likening the groups' tactics to that of Golden Dawn. "They go against the migrants . . . and then claim they were protecting [Italians] from an invasion of immigrants."

When I met him days earlier, Simone Di Stefano, CasaPound's vice president and candidate for prime minister, claimed that that "problems come from too many immigrants being present . . . and there is a feeling that immigrants are preferred by the state over Italians." "Of course, new arrivals have to be stopped, but fake refugees should be sent back. They cannot find a job [and] a house, here [in Italy]," he argued. "It doesn't make sense for them to stay because they're not entitled to be here."

CasaPound staged numerous antimigrant protests across the country. In 2017, the fascist party sparked outrage when it plastered thousands of antimigrant posters on the walls of several cities, among them Rome, Milan, and Venice. In October that same year, Forza Nuova also fueled xenophobia when it hung up posters of a black man ostensibly abusing a white woman. "Protect her from the invaders," the propaganda read. "It could be your mother wife, sister, daughter."

Antimigrant themes were far from limited to CasaPound and Forza Nuova. Mainstream right-wing parties, such as the League (also known as the Northern League), had employed xenophobic rhetoric with success. During the 2013 elections, the League secured thirteen seats in the Chamber of Deputies and twenty in the Senate. Hoping to capitalize on growing frustration, Matteo

Salvini told an election rally in December 2017 that if he won the upcoming vote, his government would provide many refugees and migrants with "a one-way ticket to send them back" to their countries. On March 5, 2018, a far-right coalition including the League, Brothers of Italy, and Forza Italia shocked much of Italy when it garnered a strong showing in the national elections. A couple months later, in May, it was in discussions with the antiestablishment, populist Five Star Movement to form a government.

The previous government under the leadership of the Democratic Party, which was headed by former center-left prime minister Matteo Renzi (2014–2016), has also done its part to create a hostile environment for refugees and migrants. During his first eight months in office, Marco Minniti, the Italian interior minister, oversaw policies that led to an 87 percent decrease in arrivals. As a result of Italian and European Union policies, some eighteen thousand refugees and migrants were trapped in Libya, a war-torn country where many of them were forced into open slave markets and torture had become widespread.

Back in Baobab Experience, nightfall came, and the camp swelled with people coming for a hot meal and a place to sleep without harassment by authorities. Although 125 people were there when I visited, volunteers and solidarity activists said the number of inhabitants in the camp often tops 500 during warmer weather. Flames danced from the smoldering wood panels on the ground in front of a zigzag of makeshift tents, many of them dimly illuminated by the light of cellphones inside, others dark and quiet. Inside a large white tent, lit by a generator, a handful of young men charged their phones at a bundle of wires and outlets in the far corner. Flags were sketched in marker up and down the tarpaulin walls—Egypt, Syria, Tunisia, Eritrea, Sudan, and Somalia, among others. Andrea Costa, one of the founding activists of Baobab Experience, sat at a makeshift table of plywood propped up on cinder blocks, describing the camp's work as part of the "anti-fascist struggle."

Baobab Experience provided a number of services: immigration information to people passing through, food, clothing, medicine, language courses, and tours of Rome. For Costa, this work was part of a political project to fight back against growing anti-migrant sentiment. Far-right groups had repeatedly staged protests outside of Baobab Experience and took to social media to falsely accuse Costa and others—who carry out their work on a volunteer basis—of making a lucrative profit by working with refugees and migrants. "We've had many problems with fascists, but, fortunately, we responded to the fascist provocations by . . . insisting that we are not doing anything wrong and that big parts of the city are standing with us," he said. "We've handled it well, but we have to tell migrants to keep an eye out when they are coming and going, to be safe." Flicking the ash of his cigarette onto the pavement, he concluded: "We are very afraid because we are getting near the elections and it seems that all of the political parties . . . want to show they are tough on migration [in order] to get more votes."

Outside, Ali sat next to the campfire under the twilit sky, ribbons of wraithlike smoke floating upward in front of him before disintegrating into the night. He shook his head in disappointment and slipped on a weatherworn red beanie, pulling it down to his eyebrows. The teenager said he hoped to move elsewhere in Europe. Explaining that he had provided his fingerprints in Italy as part of the Dublin regulations, he said that he would go back to Sudan if he is eventually returned to Italy. An austere expression across his face, he concludes: "We didn't expect Europe to be like this."

"WAR" ON JOURNALISTS

In December 2017, around ten far-right activists from Forza Nuova, an Italian neofascist party, converged on the offices of *La Repubblica* and *L'Espresso*, a pair of Italian newspapers that share offices on the outskirts of Rome. Donning white masks and hoodies, the neofascists held banners and chanted slogans against the newspaper before hurling flares at the building and at staff members standing outside. Reading a confusing and rambling communique, the far-rightists declared a "war" on the newspapers.

Alessandra Paolini, one of the journalists present during the assault, recalled the incident a month later. "They pulled out banners, yelled, and read a statement that was impossible to understand," she recounted. "Then they ran away. Afterwards, we received many threats on Facebook. They insisted that 'this is not over.'" Forza Nuova subsequently took to Facebook to reiterate its "declaration of war" against left-wing and liberal media outlets, which it claimed were operated by "terrorists masquerading as journalists."[3]

Forza Nuova was founded in 1997 by Roberto Fiore, a self-proclaimed fascist who had to flee Italy in the 1980s after his office was raided and police found explosives and weapons, and Massimo Morsello, a fascist politician and songwriter believed to have been a member of a far-right terrorist organization in the 1970s.

For Federica Angeli, another journalist at *La Repubblica*, the threats Forza Nuova issued in December were nothing new. Angeli had long been the target of far-right groups, among them CasaPound and Forza Nuova, and their mafia affiliates. In 2013, Angeli was working on an investigation that found that a Casa-Pound member, a member of the Spada Clan mafia network, and an army officer had gone in together in a joint business, a nightclub, in Ostia. "For two hours, Spada told me he would kill me, he would kill my babies, that he knows me," Angeli, an Ostia resident, said. "He told me to forget the story about the beach club, to forget about CasaPound and Spada being together in business. Only when my colleagues showed them that the camera was not recording, they decided to let me go. But everything was recording."

Shaken but defiant, Angeli soon found that the incident would not be her last run-in with the far right and the mafia. In 2016, Roberto Spada hosted a party in a central square in Ostia. The square, she recalled, was completely covered in banners and posters supporting CasaPound. After she published a story about the event, the Spada threats started again. On Facebook, Casa-Pound supporters flooded her page with threats. "They said: 'You're a bitch. You're a fucking communist. I will kill you.' Everything." Among those who personally threatened Angeli was Luca Marsella, the leader of CasaPound's Ostia chapter. Marsella became a district councillor in November 2017 when the party clinched 9 percent of the municipal vote in Ostia. In another instance, one of the Spada members spotted Angeli while she was sitting in a café and stopped at her table. Silently, he stood over her baby's stroller and made the sign of the cross.

THE CERVI BROTHERS

On the morning of December 28, 1943, Italian soldiers dragged the seven Cervi brothers from the jail cells where they had been detained for more than a month and led them to the outskirts of town.[4] A firing squad raised their weapons and shot them down, leaving their bodies lifeless on the cold earth. The Cervi brothers were infamous anti-fascists who had led the local peasant resistance to dictator Benito Mussolini's rule. They had been arrested a month earlier after fascist forces surrounded their farmhouse, setting it ablaze and forcing the men to surrender. They were not allotted a proper burial until October 1945, five months after the last vestiges of Italian fascism were toppled. With thousands of locals following behind their flag-draped coffins during the funeral, their father Alcide uttered a sentence that later became ingrained into the national consciousness: "After one harvest there comes another."

Meeting me on a chilly morning in early January 2018, Adelmo, the now seventy-four-year-old son of Aldo Cervi, who was shot dead nearly seventy-five years ago with his brothers, sauntered through the cemetery where they are buried. Only four months old at the time of their murder, Adelmo couldn't remember his father or his uncles. Yet, his entire life has been sculpted by their legacy of resistance to authoritarianism and fascism, he said. "I only come here when there are official ceremonies," he said. "I don't believe in cemeteries. If I want to speak to them, I look at their photos and remember their story." With a full head of gray hair and a thick, unkempt beard, Adelmo spent decades working to keep their memory alive. In recent years, he had also been a leading voice against the rise of neofascist parties as a surge in far-right activity gripped Italy.

Although parties such as CasaPound and Forza Nuova remain comparatively small, researchers and experts insist that they command an increasingly profound influence on the national discourse. Daniele Albertazzi, a senior lecturer in European politics at the U.K.-based Birmingham University, said in an interview that "they do have an important impact on the discourse because their discourse is now being repeated by much larger parties," referring to the extreme anti-immigrant policy proposals of the League and others like it.

"What is clear is that certain ideas are now mainstream, and they are mainstream also because of the inability of the left to have any kind of narrative or anything to say about migration," Albertazzi told me. "So, these ideas are the only ones being heard." "The whole issue of migration is completely framed by the right," he explained. Despite laws against the open promulgation of fascism in Italy, CasaPound and Forza Nuova were able to proudly identify as such without repercussions from the state. "The space of those who don't want to call themselves fascists but still hate immigrants is completely occupied by the Northern League," Albertazzi said. "So, they don't shy away from calling themselves fascists."

Just a week before I met Adelmo, upward of five thousand CasaPound supporters assembled in central Rome, marching through the capital in a neatly organized, military-like fashion. On February 3, a far-right assailant opened fire on a group of African migrants in Macerata, a small city in central Italy. It marked the 142nd attack by neofascist groups since 2014.[5] A week later, several thousand anti-fascists and antiracists stormed the streets to rally against the rise of the far right. "If we give them space today, then they will grow and grow in the future," Adelmo argued. "It would be a tragedy for all of the people who died to bring democracy to this country."

That tragedy was deeply personal for people like Cervi, who was raised by his grandfather, Alcide, and mother after his father's murder. Alcide had been a conservative Catholic until he found himself imprisoned by fascist authorities. During his time in lockup in the early 1930s, he became a communist and believer in militant anti-fascism. After his release, Alcide worked to instill anti-fascist values in his children, who eventually grew up to fight against the dictatorship. From their modest farmhouse, they printed and distributed anti-Mussolini propaganda and harbored anti-fascist fighters and dissident intellectuals.

In July 1943, the townspeople of Reggio Emilia gathered in the square to celebrate after learning from the radio that Mussolini had been dismissed and arrested. The Cervi family joined the festivities and passed out a celebratory pasta dish to locals. Yet, fascism had not entirely collapsed. Two months later, Mussolini was rescued by German forces. German leader Adolf Hitler planned to arrest the king and restore Mussolini's rule over the war-ravaged country. Instead, the king fled south and Mussolini subsequently declared the Italian Social Republic, effectively a Nazi satellite state, in the German-occupied parts of the country, which included Reggio Emilia.

The Cervi brothers, who had been sheltering anti-fascist dissidents and fighters in their home for years, retreated to the mountains near Reggio to set up partisan units to fight fascist forces and their German backers. In November, fascist forces surrounded the Cervi family's farm after they returned to Reggio Emilia. "It was considered a place for bandits and criminals," Adelmo explained. "It was all very hard on my grandmother," Adelmo said. "Aside from losing her children, the house was burned down several times," he recounted. "They not only killed my father and my uncles—they killed by grandmother.... She died of a broken heart shortly after."

Almost a year and a half later, on April 25, 1945, the National Liberation Committee of Northern Italy announced that it had taken the remaining swaths of the country back from fascist forces and issued death sentences for the entirety of the fascist leadership. Three days later, Mussolini was shot dead.

While Adelmo's family became a national symbol of resistance, they continued to live an impoverished life. Adelmo dropped out of school before graduating to help his grandfather on their farm. "When I was four or five years old, I remember my grandfather having people over and telling people the story of my father and uncles," he recalled. "People always talk about the factory workers, but no one talks about the peasants."

For Albertina Soliani, president of the Cervi Institute, the seven brothers represented the often-overlooked role of rural communities in the resistance to Mussolini's regime. "The main push was dignity," she said, sitting in the institute's library, which is located next to the farmhouse that is now a museum. "To understand resistance, we have to understand how fascism was born: It came from the conservative people who were rich and obtained power." Explaining that the "resistance came in all forms, in the rural areas and up in the mountains" and was comprised of "Italians and foreigners," she added: "It wasn't just the intellectuals and the bourgeoise [in the cities]." Soliani said: "In the rural world, people fought for peace and solidarity. Their aspirations were to be independent. . . . And they gave dignity to the rural [Italians]."

In the years following Italy's liberation, the Cervi brothers' story became part of the national mythology of anti-fascism and democracy. In 1968, the family's legacy was enshrined in the film *The Seven Cervi Brothers*. "It's not only the story of this family— it's the story of the people," Soliani concluded.

FIGHTING FASCISM TODAY

With groups like CasaPound and Forza Nuova on the rise, Adelmo has become increasingly active in anti-fascist projects and education initiatives in recent years. Adelmo regularly travels the country to speak at demonstrations, at public schools, in universities, and in debates. In addition to advocating for the rights of refugees and migrants, he also tracks down young people who are involved in CasaPound and Forza Nuova to warn them of the dangers far-right groups pose to the country's democracy.

Adelmo argues that the most important role the older generations can play in fighting contemporary fascism is educating young people to prevent the rise of conditions favorable to the far right. "Many of the kids in the younger generation don't know the history and don't understand the dangers of what happened," he said. "I've met many teachers that don't understand this part of our history."

For his part, Cervi stresses the role of capitalism in creating the conditions for fascism. Without an effective alternative to the far right, Adelmo fears for the fate of future generations. "These new movements, of course, use populism and claim they are against capitalism," he said. Against this backdrop, he laments the failure of the institutional left to address the growing inequity and socioeconomic problems working-class Italians endure. "These new fascist groups run in elections, but they shouldn't be allowed to run in the elections," he said. "After the sacrifices made by people like my family, groups like Forza Nuova and CasaPound should not be allowed to exist." "We need to listen to the needs of the people," he concluded, "because my father and uncles—like others—paid a very heavy price for fighting fascism. . . . If we allow them to continue, we can't cry afterwards."

"I DID NOT COME WITH A BOUQUET OF FLOWERS"

Italy's anti-fascist movement has existed since the advent of fascism itself. Anarchists, syndicalists, communists, socialists, and others rallied and organized against fascist violence since the inception of Benito Mussolini's authoritarian movement.

One of the first documented attacks by fascists on leftists came on April 15, 1919, when Mussolini's supporters targeted the Italian Socialist Party's *Avanti* newspaper in Milan. Angry over the outcome of the First World War, fascists gained momentum in Italy, focusing their ire on the left and on anarchists.

Mussolini, a former socialist, unionist, and war veteran, was changed by the war and what he viewed as the betrayal of the nation and its troops. Drawing from Greek philosophers, Germany's Friedrich Nietzsche, and economist Vilfredo Pareto, among others, Mussolini built a new alternative rooted in ultranationalism, national syndicalism, biological racialism, and Italian expansionism overseen by an all-powerful, totalitarian regime.

In 1921, with fascism on the rise, a broad umbrella of left-wing and anarchist groups created the People's Militia. However, they were unable to prevent Mussolini's seizure of power, which came the following year when the fascists infamously marched on Rome and launched a coup. Just two months later, fascists initiated a brutal, three-day assault on the labor movement in Turin, rounding up communists and trade unionists and killing at least eleven people.

In 1924, Amerigo Dumini, a member of the fascist secret police, assassinated Socialist Party leader Giacomo Matteotti, stabbing him to death in a car and dumping his body in Riano, located about fourteen miles outside Rome. As an act of revenge, anti-fascist Giovanni Corvi killed Armando Casalini, a fascist deputy, on a train in September 1924. Tit-for-tat violence continued largely unabated, with anti-fascists defending their communities to the best of their abilities.

Mussolini himself was the target of numerous assassination attempts. On September 11, 1926, anarchist Gino Lucetti threw a bomb at the leader's car in Rome.[6] The attempt on Mussolini's life was unsuccessful—the bomb bounced off the car and injured others. Under interrogation, Lucetti reportedly said: "I did not come with a bouquet of flowers for Mussolini. I was willing to use my pistol if I had not achieved my aim with the bomb." He was later sentenced to thirty years in prison, from which he escaped with the help of comrades in 1943, only to be killed by German bombing shortly after. Another attempt came in October 1926, when fifteen-year-old anarchist Anteo Zamboni opened fire in Mussolini's direction during a parade in Bologna. When the shots missed, the boy was seized by fascist squads, who lynched and killed him there in the streets.

In November 1936, with the Second World War looming, Mussolini changed his tune on Nazi Germany, the expansion of which he'd previously opposed, and signed the first pact with Hitler's regime. The following year, Japan, Germany, and Italy signed the Anti-Comintern Pact, an alliance conceived to oppose the spread of communism. Nonetheless, Mussolini proclaimed Italy's neutrality in 1939 when Germany invaded Poland. In 1940, Italy joined the war on the side of Germany and the Axis Powers.

Aldo Tortorella was born on July 10, 1926, to a bourgeoise family. While in high school, he said, he developed anti-fascist politics owing to a philosophy teacher who taught subversive texts. Although the teacher could not openly encourage the students to oppose fascism, he regularly assigned anti-fascist readings, mostly communist and socialist theory. "Having grown up in a conservative family, it opened my mind to a communist worldview," the ninety-one-year-old Tortorella explained when I met him in his home in Rome in January 2018. Also during high school, he befriended a young man who worked in a publishing house.

"He used to print out the pope's speeches," he recalled. "By reading his anticommunist speeches, I became more interested and convinced," he said, the sentence giving way to laughter.

In Milan, as a university student just seventeen years old in 1943, Tortorella joined the Italian Communist Party and joined the partisan movement to fight the fascist regime. First tasked with establishing the Youth Front, a group of anti-fascist and left-wing teenagers working against the regime, their activities focused on organizing strikes, distributing anti-fascist literature, and working with factory employees. "There was a rule that we weren't supposed to take up weapons because we were minors," Tortorella said. "But it wasn't long before we took up arms."

Tortorella and his comrades began carrying out ambushes on fascist squadrons in Milan and attacking the regime's weapons depots. "First, we were sabotaging the weapons, ruining them so that they couldn't be fired," he said. "We were putting nails in the streets so that fascist vehicles couldn't enter our neighborhoods. We also blew up train tracks to stop the delivery of more weapons, when we could." Eventually, their ambushes on weapons depots became acts of seizure. "We were stealing the weapons and building up our arms," he said. "But the battle itself was a minimal part of what we did. We would have gotten nowhere if we hadn't built an anti-fascist consensus among the community. We were talking to the people and building a mass organization."

That same year, fascist authorities captured and arrested the teenager. After being held in detention for months, he was able to escape with the help of comrades. "I hid in a college for nurses," Tortorella remembered. "The nuns and students there knew who I was, but no one said a word. The fascists were searching for me everywhere, but no one spoke."

In July 1943, Mussolini was dismissed and arrested. Still underground, Tortorella came out of hiding briefly to join in when Milan residents toppled a statue of the fascist leader. He was subsequently sent to Genoa, where he joined the partisans on the front lines, fighting the fascist regime and its German backers. "Most of our leaders had been jailed or killed, so I went there to reorganize the Youth Front," he said. "The fighting was brutal."

In 1945, when the regime was finally toppled, he was stuck in the communist newspaper's headquarters writing about the event. "I was writing about our liberation, taking lines from comrades on the front lines, but I didn't get to see any of it," he said, holding up a copy of the newspaper bearing the article he wrote that night. "I spent the night on the phone taking news lines. That night, I described the liberation, but I hadn't seen anything." After the war, Tortorella became a leading editorial figure in *L'Unita*, the communist party's newspaper, and eventually was elected to the Italian Chamber of Deputies for the first time in 1972.

Watching a spurt of fascist growth today, Tortorella says the youth who are vulnerable to drifting to the far right are in desperate need of alternatives. "Fascism is a reaction of the ruling classes when they cannot stand the pressure coming from the people," he argued. "Before, it was against the Jews, now it's about the immigrants ... of course, it still maintains hatred for Jews."

Tortorella argued that providing stable employment for working-class youth and educating the masses about the dangers of fascism are indispensable for preventing the rise of neofascism. "The younger generation needs stable jobs because they feel abandoned. If they feel this way, and live in precarious situations with no future, what will happen is that they can continue to join these violent fascist parties," he insisted. "Many of the younger generations who call themselves fascists don't even know what it means: They think it means order, jobs, and building cities. They forget there was no place for public discussion, that the country went backward, and they forget about all the people who died during the war. For years, anti-fascists thought it was over and made a mistake by giving space to these new groups to grow."

He blamed the postwar left for not eradicating the social conditions that pave the path toward fascism. "We thought it was over, we thought that we had won, and that it couldn't return," he lamented. "If we don't give ideals to the young people now, it could end very badly."

NOTES

1. Patrick Strickland, "Anti-fascists Vow to Fight Mussolini-Loving 'Militants,'" *Al Jazeera English,* January 21, 2018, http://www.aljazeera.com/news/2018/01/anti-fascists-vow-fight-mussolini-loving-militants-180116190056142.html.

2. Patrick Strickland, "How Italy's Far Right Exploits the Migration Crisis," *Al Jazeera English*, January 15, 2018, http://www.aljazeera.com/news/2018/01/italy-exploits-migration-crisis-180114200719130.html.

3. Jessica Phelan, "Italian Newspaper Offices Blockaded by Far-Right

Forza Nuova Party," *The Local*, December 7, 2017, https://www.thelocal.it/20171207/italy-newspaper-repubblica-espresso-forza-nuova.

4. Patrick Strickland, "Remembering Italy's Cervi Brothers amid Far-Right Surge," *Al Jazeera English*, February 19, 2018, https://www.aljazeera.com/news/2018/02/remembering-italy-cervi-brothers-surge-180213164326651.html.

5. Lorenzo Tondo, "Attacks on Immigrants Highlight Rise of Fascist Groups in Italy," *Guardian*, February 6, 2018, https://www.theguardian.com/world/2018/feb/06/attacks-on-immigrants-highlight-rise-of-fascist-groups-in-italy.

6. Pietro de Piero, "1926: The Attempted Assassination of Mussolini in Rome," *Libcom*, September 10, 2006, https://libcom.org/history/1926-attempted-assassination-mussolini.

5

CROATIA

Sitting in a friend's ninth-story flat in Novi Zagreb, a neighborhood in the Croatian capital, thirty-five-year-old Lovro Krnić dropped a stack of Antifa stickers on the cluttered coffee table in front of him. An IT employee by trade, Krnić has become an influential figure in Croatia's contemporary anti-fascist movement in recent years, taking to his website, Anti-Fascist Courier (Antifašistički Vjesnik), to expose far-right conspiracy theories and out neofascist historical revisionism.

Rolling a filterless cigarette, Krnić explained that he and his colleagues launched the Anti-Fascist Courier as a Facebook page in 2014 to commemorate the upcoming seventieth anniversary of Zagreb's liberation from fascism. "We started with writing small stories about the [Partisan] resistance in Zagreb," he said, referring to the largely communist rebellion that led to the overthrow of the Ustaše regime during the Second World War. "Then we eventually founded this site to make it a more serious operation."

The Courier's reputation as a prominent anti-fascist force in Croatia was solidified by its dogged efforts to expose and debunk the historical revisionism prominent on Croatia's far-right, which had found an eager ear in the corridors of power in recent years. "After years and years of lies, people start to think that's it, this is just history," he said, explaining that conspiracy theories about the country's role in the Holocaust and the number of Partisans slaughtered by fascists during the war, among others, were growing increasingly popular at the time.

Raised in Šibenik, located in the country's central Dalmatia region, Krnić, who comes from a mixed Croat-Serb family, began to grow interested in the legacy of anti-fascism in Croatia and the former Yugoslavia more than a decade ago, when he visited an anti-fascist monument that had been destroyed in the Yugoslav wars of the 1990s. Aware that several of his ancestors' names were on the monument, he decided to place flowers at the base of the still-standing—but badly damaged—plaque at the foot of where the monument used to stand. "Everybody was afraid to do that," he recalled, explaining that the intense nationalism that gripped the country in the wake of the 1990s war had resulted in widespread fear of openly celebrating the Partisans' legacy. "Some of my family members were even afraid for my life."

His grandmother, who is of Orthodox and Serb ancestry, issued several warnings to Krnić, recalling the threats she endured during the Croatian-Yugoslav war, when anti-Serb militias and the Croatian army took control of their hometown in September 1991. "Many older people, and people who love me, were afraid for my life," he recollected. "People told my grandmother [during the war] that Ustaše [the Second World War–era fascists in Croatia] is now in power."

"My grandfather's name and that of several other distant relatives are on the plaque," he explained. "There are bullet holes on it, but you can still see the names."

That experience started a process in Krnić, one that made him devote himself to anti-fascism.

Krnić's work at the Courier brought threats of violence. In 2017, when activists protested proposals to reinstate mandatory military conscription, he noticed that right-wing counterprotesters —sniper veterans from the 1990s' war—had worn insignia bearing German Nazi markings from the Schutzstaffel paramilitary (also known as the SS). After spotting the symbol while pouring through photos from the protest and counterdemonstration, Krnić researched the origins of the SS insignia and published an article at the Courier detailing its history. Threats immediately poured into the page's Facebook inbox and were posted as comments under the link to the article. "They were openly threatening us on Facebook," he said. "It's pretty frightening to get threats from snipers."

In 2016, Croatian filmmaker Jakov Sedlar premiered *Jasenovac—The Truth*, a documentary film premised on hoax theories about the role of the Ustaše in the genocide of the Holocaust. Although most scholars agree that upwards of eighty-two thousand Serbs, Jews, Roma, and anti-fascists were murdered in Jasenovac, the country's largest extermination camp, between 1941 and 1945, Sedlar's film argued that the true death toll never exceeded eighteen thousand. Further, Sedlar claimed that the Yugoslav communist government, under the leadership of Josip Broz Tito, continued to operate the camp after the war's conclusion and that most of the murders took place under communist oversight. The director offered shots of newspaper front pages and supposedly official documents to support the documentary's claims. The film concluded with a narrator deeming the Partisan resistance "liberal fascists."

Krnić set out to debunk the conspiracies. He went to the national library and obtained the newspaper editions by matching the publication and date to those presented in the documentary. He dredged through official documents. What he found and later published on the Courier was a simple case of eighteen blatant falsehoods, many of them achieved through photoshopping newspaper headlines. "They're always trying to fake history and demonize the Partisan movement in Croatia, and the numbers of victims of fascism, which every day are getting smaller," Krnić said. "Nobody is fighting this." "It was hard work. I had to find rare images and documents and the discrepancies [from what was presented in the film]," he added. "They were totally photoshopped, with different headlines on the newspapers. I was looking at headlines and noticing different fonts, so I had been suspicious. I was looking and seeing new Arial fonts on newspapers from World War Two."

Jasenovac—The Truth was just one development in a broader process of historical revisionism that has continually grown in recent years. In January 2016, the Croatian parliament voted to reintroduce its support for officially commemorating the killings of Ustaše fighters and civilians who accompanied them when they surrendered to British forces in Bleiburg, Austria, on May 15, 1945.[1] They were transferred to the control of the Yugoslav Partisans, and an unknown number—some estimates put it at thirty thousand—were killed. When the vote was made in 2016, it came just four years after the parliamentary presidency revoked its support for the commemoration.

FORMER WHITE NATIONALIST TURNED ANTI-FASCIST

Antonio, a twenty-one-year-old who asked me not to use his surname for his family's safety, stood behind the bar at the left-wing pub where he worked in Zagreb. With a shaved head and a soft-spoken manner, he recalled his arduous transformation from a white nationalist to an anti-fascist.

When he was fifteen years old, Antonio joined a ragtag band of white nationalists in Split, the Dalmatian city on the Adriatic coast. Influenced by the far-right movements within the Oi! music scene and widespread among soccer hooligans, he followed his brother's footsteps and found himself regularly attending white nationalist demonstrations and meet-ups. Full of resentment due to the government's failure to provide his family with welfare they were entitled to after his father's service in the Croatian army during the 1990s' Yugoslav war, his brother had fallen under the sway of white nationalists, adorned himself with a swastika tattoo, and became involved in one of the first racist skinhead groups in the city. "It all comes from some sort of anger about the country not being great," Antonio said. "That was our opinion. We were just angry, and we blamed Roma for taking our jobs and such shit. It wasn't really ever happening. We also blamed Albanians, so they were among our primary targets.

There were like five Chinese people working in a shop in Split, and they were our main target to crush."

On his eighteenth birthday, Antonio and a handful of his fellow neofascists took to the streets, drunk and angry, and staged an impromptu march in the center of Split. When they encountered a Korean man making his way home, Antonio pounced on him, beating his face and torso until police eventually arrived and hauled him off. "It was just because he looked different than me," he recalled. He was sentenced to sixty days in jail. While in lockup, he said, fellow inmates treated him "like a king." Impressed by his attack, they praised him as a model young man. "When I was in prison, when I told [other prisoners] I beat up an Asian, they looked at me like I was god. I felt good in prison because they treated me like an idol."

However, a friend in an adjacent cell recommended that he watch *American History X*, the 1998 drama that tells the tale of white supremacists in Venice, California. In that film, Edward Norton's character, Derek Vinyard, goes to prison for three years after fatally curb-stomping an African American. His younger brother, Danny, was inspired by his actions and joined the same neo-Nazi outfit, the Disciples of Christ. After Derek's release from jail, he persuades Danny not to follow in his footsteps. The film ends when, after completing a school assignment on why Nazism and racism were misguided and flawed approaches to society's ills, Danny is tragically killed. For Antonio, who watched the film "five times" the first week after his own release, the film touched close to home. "Now I can teach my younger brother not to follow my path," Antonio said. "He started to listen to punk, just like me and my older brother, and is hanging out at the same places. But he's totally different and learned from our examples."

Not content with merely preventing his brother from repeating his mistakes, Antonio moved to Zagreb and began organizing in anti-fascist circles: anti-fascist protests, demonstrations against proposals to reintroduce mandatory military conscription in Croatia, and efforts to counter Second World War historical revisionism. Pouring a drink behind the bar, he lifted his sleeve to show a tattoo: a silhouette of a Trojan-like helmet based on the logo of Skinheads Against Racial Prejudice (SHARP), the movement founded in the United Kingdom and later imported to the United States in 1987 to oppose the racist and neofascist tendencies inside the skinhead music scene. "I'm only twenty-one years old, but I feel like I'm forty now," Antonio concluded. "I've lived a lot in my life. I wasn't just tolerated [as a white nationalist] in my community. Now, when I go back, no one wants to speak to me, no one wants to sit with me and have a drink."

BATTLEFIELD OF MONUMENTS

With Croatia's far right busy burning newspapers, and the government whitewashing the crimes of the fascist-aligned Independent State of Croatia, the assault on anti-fascist symbols, which started during the Yugoslav wars, entered its twenty-seventh year without pause. More than six thousand anti-fascist monuments were built during the communist period, but since

1991 around half of them were toppled by authorities, were destroyed, had fallen into disrepair, or were pillaged by thieves. Although the vast majority of the monuments were erected by local communities to commemorate and honor the victims of fascism, Croatia's right-wing establishment and far right attempted to paint them as nothing more than anti-Croat symbols promoting communism.

On a wintry morning in March 2018, in Petrova Gora, a rural area situated in the snowy, mountainous region bordering Bosnia, the immense monument that was completed in 1981 now looked like a decaying shell of an abandoned spaceship, many of its steel panels missing. Spray-painted on the wall of a restaurant where tourists ate while visiting the Petrova Gora monument was a message: "Death to fascism." The towering monument, created by Yugoslav architect Vojin Bakić, is now less a symbol of anti-fascism than a sign of the far right's successful propaganda campaign to rewrite history in favor of the Ustaše.[2] But anti-fascists and researchers have struggled to keep alive the memory of its original intent: to mourn the Croat and Serb Partisans who fell victim to the fascist violence of that period.

Sanja Horvatinčić, a Zagreb-based researcher whose Ph.D. dissertation mapped and documented the scale of destruction of anti-fascist monuments across Croatia, sat in a noisy bar on a Saturday afternoon in early March 2018. Explaining that anti-fascist monuments were destroyed in several former Yugoslav countries, she said that the breadth of destruction pales in comparison to what took place in Croatia. "Very often it's difficult to say which monuments were collateral damage during the war and which were targeted to be damaged," she said. "There were no official directives [in the Croatian army] to destroy monuments . . . but it was widespread, and it was tolerated." "You still have in Croatia today the idea that the destruction of monuments was the same as in the eastern bloc [former Soviet countries]," she added. "They were mostly erected for local heroes or victims. So, all of the monuments in small villages had the names of families in the local communities. It's difficult to believe those people would want the monuments destroyed."

Just three days before I met Horvatinčić, thieves stole the bust of Ivo Lola Ribar, a Yugoslav communist and Partisan who was slain during Germany's bombing of the Glamoč airfield in southwestern Bosnia in 1943. His brother was also killed on the battlefield, and his fiancé, Sloboda Trajković, was gassed to death in Serbia's Banjica concentration camp the following year. For years, Croatian nationalists had advocated for Lola Ribar's bust to be removed from Barun Filipović Park in Zagreb. "This is a new wave of ideological conflict," Horvatinčić said. "Now, it is more clearly ideologically motivated than during the Yugoslav wars. . . . It's quite clear: now, are you on the side of fascists or the anti-fascists."

Meanwhile, the far right worked diligently to replace anti-fascist symbols with their own. In Drage, near sites of fierce Partisan resistance during the Second World War, relatives of convicted sectarian terrorist Miro Barešić erected a statue in his honor.[3] "Miro Barešić is one of the greatest Croatian patriots whose work and sacrifice we have to respect," Tomo Medved, the outgoing minister for war veterans in Croatia, declared at a ceremony for the statue's unveiling. He continued:

> For years, in the diaspora and in the Homeland War, he fought for a free and an independent Croatia and never gave up on his ideas, although he felt the injustice that was systematically inflicted on Croats. Like many other emigrants, who were willing to give their lives for Croatia, he was a defender before defenders. He returned from Paraguay, even though he knew that in Croatia there are people who persecuted him, but he participated in the war and experienced the realization of his dream. Thank you, Miro, for an independent, sovereign and free Croatia.

Barešić was a member of the Croatian National Resistance, a Ustaše organization founded in Spain after the Second World War. In 1971, he and three accomplices murdered Yugoslav ambassador to Sweden Vladimir Rolović. Swedish authorities sentenced him to life in prison, but he was released as part of a hostage release deal when a Scandinavian Airlines flight was hijacked by armed Croatian ultranationalists the following year.

In 1991, as Yugoslavia was being torn apart by armed conflict, Barešić returned to Croatia and took up arms. He was killed by Serb rebels that same year. "I deeply believe that Miro was never a terrorist, and no Ustaše. . . . But he was a Croatian nationalist and a freedom fighter for the Croatian state. And whoever thinks differently isn't telling the truth," Ante Barešić, the late terrorist's cousin, told the Croatian daily *Slobodna Dalmacija* at the time. The monument was Ante's idea. While Croatia's government tried to wash its hands of any responsibility in the affair by pointing to the fact that the monument was initiated by Barešić's relatives, Medved was joined by then minister of culture Zlatka Hasanbegović, known for neo-Ustaše gestures, and Dražen Keleminec, leader of the Autochthonous Croatian Party of Right (A-HSP), a far-right group.

Anti-fascists responded quickly to the monument's inauguration. Within a week of the ceremony, under the cover of night, a group of activists painted the hand of Barešić red. Although it was unclear at the time who carried out the act, Antifa Šibenik, a collective in a nearby town, posted a photo of the defaced monument on Facebook along with a post that read: "We received a photo of a completed monument to the Ustaše killer Miro Barešić."

The direct action sparked a stream of steady death threats, and police launched an investigation into the incident. "Barešić did everything that terrorists do, and now he's a hero [for Croatian ultranationalists]," Josip, one of the activists who splattered red paint on the statue, told me, speaking with a pseudonym. "At first, we did not want to publish the photos because we were waiting for their response. But they didn't want to publicly say that it happened because they were embarrassed." "After waiting, we passed it on to Antifa Šibenik to post on Facebook. We told them the monument was now finally finished," Josip said. Antifa Šibenik, who spoke to me as a collective, recalled the fiery response. "We got a death threat something like every five minutes for the five days that followed," the group said. "We had a bounty on our heads."

With a flurry of anger stoked by far-right journalists, police swiftly launched an investigation into the incident. "It was part of this narrative that they're pushing, that Antifa is an extremist organization, but they still can't produce any evidence," Antifa Šibenik told me. Although their actions have been limited to symbolic acts of rebellion and anti-fascist graffiti, anti-fascists were fighting in every way they could. "We are fighting the story of equating neo-Nazism with anti-fascism," Josip said. "We have to fight the story of revisionism, the notion that everything associated with anti-fascism has to be destroyed."

GENOCIDE

Croatia's Ustaše was an ultranationalist and fascist terrorist organization founded in 1929 and that eventually came to power when it established the Independent State of Croatia (NDH) in 1941, with the backing of Hitler's Nazi regime. The NDH functioned largely as a Nazi satellite state during the Second World War, when Ustaše members murdered hundreds of thousands of Serbs, Jews, Roma, and anti-fascists, among others. Backed by the Catholic Church and under the leadership of Ante Pavelić, a Croatian fascist who spent years in exile until the NDH's establishment, the Ustaše enacted Third Reich–inspired race laws aimed at creating an "ethnically pure" Croatia and built several concentration camps throughout the country's territory.

The NDH's main target was the country's Serb minority. In May 1941, Ustaše ministers Mile Budak, Mirko Puk, and Milovan Žanić declared that a third of Serbs would be converted, a third cleansed from the country, and a third killed. According to the U.S. Holocaust Museum, the Ustaše killed between 330,000 and 390,000 Serbs during its brutal reign.

In the end, the Ustaše met the same fate as fascists across Europe during the Second World War. The Yugoslav Partisan movement, or National Liberation Army, was led by Josip Broz Tito, the charismatic leader who later ruled the Yugoslav communist regime from 1945 until his death in 1980. Founded in 1941, the Partisan movement waged a successful war that resulted in the expulsion of fascist forces from the entirety of Yugoslavia, which includes the present-day territories of Slovenia, Croatia, Serbia, Bosnia, Montenegro, Kosovo, and Macedonia. The Socialist Federation of Yugoslav Republics existed until 1992, but, after Tito's death in 1980, the republics saw a surge in nationalist and ethnic tensions that laid the path for the bloody Yugoslav wars of the 1990s, during which the federation disintegrated into national territories.

In the late 1980s, with the Yugoslav government moving away from communism and undergoing a process of liberalization, nationalism found its grip on the ethnic communities that once lived in relative harmony under Tito's rule. Under the rule of Slobodan Milošević, the Yugoslav army was transformed into a vehicle for Serb nationalism. For Croatia, that process translated into a prolonged war. With ethnic tensions soaring, Serbs in Croatia started to take steps toward separating from the republic in 1991. Facing backlash from the increasingly nationalistic Croat leadership in Zagreb, many Serbs in the country found themselves caught in the crossfire of two competing ultranationalistic forces. On May 19, 1991, Croatia held a referendum on independence, which passed by a massive 94 percent vote. Serbs in Croatia had boycotted the vote. Characterized by massive human rights violations and widespread war crimes, the war, which eventually led to the collapse of Yugoslavia and the establishment of an independent Croatian state, stretched on until 1995. Tens of thousands of people were killed, and an estimated five hundred thousand became refugees or internally displaced persons. Hailed as the "Homeland War" in Croatia, the conflict saw the resurrection of Ustaše and fascist themes in Croatia.

THE UNEXPECTED RETURN OF FASCISM

Born in 1944 in Zagreb, Zoran Pusić was among the most active and vocal opponents of the neofascism gripping Croatia in the 1990s. Largely apolitical at the time, he was walking in central Zagreb one day in the mid-1970s when he stumbled upon graffiti that declared: "Death to fascism! Freedom to the people!" Sitting in his office in March 2018, he recalled feelings of confusion when he saw the slogan tagged on the wall. "It felt very out of place," he said. "I thought there was no fascism, but there are a lot of problems that we should certainly move to resolving, including the need for a more democratic society." Later that night, he returned to the spot, and below the graffiti he spray-painted the infamous Partisan slogan: "Down with Franz Josef!" Josef was the emperor of Austria, the king of Hungary, and monarch of a handful of other states in the Austro-Hungarian Empire. "I just wanted to show how out of place it was," Pusić said.

Yet, less than two decades later, Pusić was shocked to see the resurrection of neo-Ustaše ideology. With nationalism rising and Yugoslavia speeding toward its bloody collapse, he started to notice Ustaše graffiti on the walls of Zagreb and other Croatian cities. "Little by little, Milošević's ire was turned toward other communist republics in Yugoslavia," he remembered. "This strongly influenced the development of Croatian nationalism at the time."

In June 1989, the Croatian Democratic Union (HDZ) was founded as a nationalist alternative to communist rule. "From the beginning, I was quite afraid of the nationalism of HDZ and other directly pro-Ustaše parties," he said. The right-wing HDZ remains an umbrella party that provides a comfortable home for neofascist and far-right factions. "Political pluralism was really just in front of us [in the 1990s], but at the same time, nationalism in Serbia was growing stronger and stronger. . . . At the beginning it was pointed against the Albanian political leadership in Kosovo, but little by little, it was turned toward other republics from Slovenia to Bosnia to Croatia."

Under the leadership of Frano Tudman, a longtime Croatian right-wing dissident, HDZ was the main force in Croatia as the war approached. Tudman was known for making anti-Serb state-

ments and praising what he deemed the positive aspects of genocide. In 1992, the HDZ won parliamentary elections, and the landslide of racism and sectarianism gained yet more speed. Changing the largely symbolic designation of the country's Serb
population from a "nation" to an "ethnic minority" was only one
of several moves made by the newly inaugurated right-wing
leadership that poured fuel on the flames of nationalism.

The introduction of anti-Serb policies was accompanied by a
concerted effort to distort the legacy of Yugoslavia's Partisan
movement. The names of squares and streets affiliated with
the Partisan resistance began to be changed. The Victims of Fascism Square, situated in central Zagreb, was renamed Croatian
Nobles' Square in 1990. Appalled by the move, Pusić and others
started to organize. Not a communist himself, Pusić nonetheless
believed in the Yugoslav communist mantra "brotherhood and
unity" and understood the renaming to be an attempt to white-
wash Croatia's role in the Holocaust and wartime European fascism.

One day shortly after a new sign proclaiming the central area
to be "Croatian Nobles' Square" was erected, Pusić painted over
it, replacing "nobles" with "dwarfs." Along with other activists,
Pusić established a committee to return the square to its previous name. They began to publish articles in the local press and
to organize commemorations for the May 9 Victory Day, which is
marked annually to celebrate the defeat of the Axis forces during
the Second World War. "The name had been changed under the
direct order of Tudman," he said. "We immediately started acting

against it." On May 9, 1991, Pusić and other activists assembled in the square and staged a protest. Such rallies were unpopular amid the fervent nativism gripping the country, he said. They began to organize forums, shadow parliaments, and other platforms to oppose nationalism and war. The Croatia-based activists also built ties with antiwar activists in other parts of Yugoslavia. "We did a lot, but we were not strong enough to stop it."

With the prospect of war looming, Pusić sent his sixteen-year-old son to New York to stay with family friends. Meanwhile, at home, he continued to rally and organize against the violations of human rights that were spiraling out of control. In 1992, with Croatian authorities and militiamen carrying out a campaign of home evictions targeting Serbs, Pusić and others employed a combination of negotiations and nonviolent direct actions, such as sit-ins, to prevent the evictions. "A lot of people [mostly Serbs and mixed Orthodox-Catholic families] who had some connection to the Yugoslav army were being kicked out of their homes," he said. Some evictions were carried out by police at the behest of the Croatian Ministry of Defense, while others were vigilante operations that saw the random expulsion of Serbs from their homes by armed men. "I witnessed between seventy and eighty of those evictions," he said of the latter. "We were doing sit-ins, arguing with police about why it was illegal, and it went on from 1992 until the end of 1994. It was very demanding activity because it was always on the verge of a direct conflict."

In one instance in 1993, Pusić arrived at an apartment in Zagreb to find a uniformed police officer with a bomb in his hand.

While a woman and her two children huddled inside, Pusić dissuaded the officer from carrying out the eviction. The following year, Pusić and other activists were conducting a five-hour sit-in outside another flat when police lost their patience and attacked them. "They attacked me . . . and several of them hit me," he recalled. "They brought me to jail afterwards. Journalists took photos, and it became a major scandal."

By the time the evictions were halted in 1997, more than ten thousand people had been evicted from their homes, according to the estimates of NGOs. In Zagreb, Pusić and fellow activists were able to prevent at least 350 evictions.[4] "Of course, this was a kind of fascism," he said of the evictions. "It was ethnic cleansing . . . and most of the war criminals from the Croatian side described themselves as fans of the Ustaše movement."

CROATIA'S ALT-RIGHT

Frano Čirko sat in an upscale café in the Croatian capital and took sips of an espresso as he boasted of founding the country's version of the "alt-right" movement.[5] Placing his coffee cup on the table and folding his hands, the twenty-eight-year-old said he founded the far-right Generation of Renovation party in February 2017 with the hopes of creating a Croatian version of the alt-right and the anti-immigrant European Identitarian movement.

Last year, two months after Generation of Renovation's establishment, the party was able to land councillors, including Čirko, in a pair of neighborhoods in western Zagreb. While Croatia's mainstream political establishment has drifted further right in recent years—a process that has seen the normalization of neo-fascist themes—Čirko and his fellow party members decided to start the new party after preexisting far-right groups effectively collapsed during parliamentary elections in 2016. "They have an old methodology of political work," he said. "They always talk about the Second World War and the Homeland War [the Yugo-slav wars in the 1990s]."

Yet, Sven Milekić, a Zagreb-based journalist at *Balkan Insight*, rejected the notion that Generation of Renovation represents a break from the country's traditional far right. "When you look at their programs, rhetoric, and membership, it's the same guys who used to look like neo-Nazis," he said. Explaining that Čirko's party has failed to gain much currency in the country, Milekić ex-plained: "In Croatia, it's very hard for new parties to step onto the scene. People are quite conservative in the sense of their po-litical choices."

The party claimed to have around two hundred members. While it had struggled to build a presence in the streets, it quickly gained notoriety for its promotion of hate speech and xenophobia online. The Generation of Renovation party has co-opted the American alt-right's Pepe the Frog, a meme described as a hate symbol by the Southern Poverty Law Center, a U.S.-based watch-dog organization. Čirko cloaks the party's far-right ideology in campaigns against youth emigration and in support of youth-fo-cused employment policies. "Old right-wing politicians are only fighting against communists, which is OK, but they aren't fighting

against the socialist way of economy and how the state is working," he says, alluding to the flight of many young Croatians to
other EU states for employment after the country joined the
twenty-eight-member bloc in 2013. Čirko described Generation
of Renovation as a youth-focused party that opposes Croatia's
membership in the EU and calls for the abolition of income taxes.
"We are fighting for the interests of our generation. . . . We are
not guilty for our situation," he argued. "We have the right to resist this situation in politics and [economics] because we were
[forced] into it."

In contrast to these claims, researchers and critics have
pointed to the party leader's long history of neofascist activism.
Čirko, who has in the past been photographed performing Nazi
salutes, is a former member of the hardline, far-right Croatian
Pure Party of Rights. He has worked to build ties with several
far-right and neofascist groups across Europe, including Hungary's Jobbik party, the Latvian National Alliance, the Conservative People's Party of Estonia, and VMRO—Bulgarian National
Movement. "We found Hungary as the first and strongest Croatian ally in our neighborhood," he explained. "Jobbik's only step
after this is to come to power." Founded in 2003, Jobbik has made
waves time and again owing to its intense Euroscepticism, antimigrant policies, and anti-Semitism. Although it has recently attempted to rebrand itself, critics point to Jobbik's neo-Nazi roots.

Pressed on his views, Čirko employed ultranationalistic
tropes, such as the notion that Croatia should be a strong country
that commands influence in the world. Although Čirko claims his

party doesn't harbor the intense anti-Serb xenophobia that is widespread in many of Croatia's right-wing and far-right parties, his actions suggest otherwise. During rallies and other public events, Čirko and his fellow party members regularly wave flags bearing symbols affiliated with the Ustaše, the Second World War–era fascist party that oversaw the Nazi-aligned Independent State of Croatia in the early 1940s.

In November 2017, a day after Bosnian Croat general Slobodan Praljak drank cyanide poison following his conviction for war crimes during the 1990s Yugoslav wars, Generation of Renovation held a ceremony and erected an altar for the late war criminal. "We have come to pay tribute to our general, Slobodan Praljak, in gratitude for all he has done for us and for all of the Croatian people," Čirko said as he addressed the handful of supporters. They held a placard that read "hero." Although publicly approving of, celebrating, or minimizing war crimes is forbidden under Croatian law, Čirko's memorial was only one of several similar displays of mourning staged throughout the country following Praljak's suicide. Some of those events were attended by government ministers.

While noting that the growing far-right ideology is "dangerous," the Anti-Fascist Network of Zagreb's Josip Jagić said he doubts that a party such as Generation of Renovation can build a large base. Jagić explained that the prevalence of Holocaust revisionism and other far-right characteristics in Croatia's ruling right-wing party, the Croatian Democratic Union (HDZ), has served as a barrier for far-right parties hoping to break into the country's political mainstream. "Because there is nothing remotely viable as a real opposition [to HDZ], which by some degree would contest the current relations of power in society, the establishment is pretty much secure," he said. "That situation means you have no need for fascist outrage," Jagić added. "We have to admit that the fascist activities have been until now on the margins." He concluded: "It's here, it's dangerous, but it still doesn't have the broad potential of fascism [elsewhere in Europe]."

BURNING PAPERS

Nikola Bajto sat in the office of *Novosti*, a left-wing Serb minority newspaper based in Zagreb, and explained the paper's long history of being attacked by right-wing and far-right public figures in Croatia. In November 2017, a group of members from the pro-Ustaše Autochthonous Croatian Party of Right (A-HSP) gathered in front of *Novosti*'s Zagreb headquarters to burn copies of the paper.[6] The far-rightists, setting papers ablaze, chanted "Za dom spremni" ("Ready for the homeland"), a Croatian version of the German Nazi slogan "sieg heil." Public burnings of the paper had started in September, two months earlier.

The A-HSP was infamous for its pro-Ustaše and neo-Nazi advocacy. After the election of U.S. president Donald Trump, thirty party members marched to the U.S. embassy in Zagreb to rally in support of Trump, who had been busy courting the support of white nationalists and neo-Nazis at home. They waved U.S. flags next to the Croatian flag and flags bearing the unofficial symbols of the Ustaše. Against this backdrop, with Donald Trump having hesitated to disavow the endorsement of former Ku Klux Klan leader David Duke, the U.S. embassy's condemnation of A-HSP's march rang hollow for anti-fascists and minorities in Croatia.

In July 2016, A-HSP members and other neofascists attempted to disrupt a ceremony to commemorate the 1941 anti-fascist uprising in Srb, a village on the border of Bosnia.[7] After being blocked from accessing the site of the event, they blocked traffic and chanted fascist slogans in unison.

A large mural of Josip Broz Tito hung from the wall behind Bajto. In an adjacent corner, a corkboard was blanketed in anti-fascist stickers. Stirring sugar into black coffee, Bajto explained that he and his colleagues had been the target of numerous threats, including death threats. In March 2018, just days before I met him, someone sent an envelope stuffed with human feces to the paper. "We were the newspaper that first wrote about the [neofascist] plaque in Jasenovac, near the concentration camp," Bajto recalled, explaining that far-right activists repeatedly accused *Novosti*'s reporters of being "anti-Croat."

In late February 2018, the government-appointed Council for Dealing with Consequences of the Rule of Non-Democratic Regimes, which was established in March 2017 to assess the legality of the plaque, came to a sobering conclusion that spoke volumes about the overlap between far-right and neo-Ustaše positions and the mainstream political establishment in Croatia.[8] "'Za dom spremni' on the Croatian Defence Forces's (HOS) coat of arms can be used only exceptionally, only in relation to those situations, sites, or cemeteries, where HOS members were killed. This permission does not change the conclusion that the slogan is unconstitutional," Zvonko Kusić, president of the council, said at a press conference at the time.

In effect, the council ruled that although the promotion of fascism was unconstitutional, it should be permitted in certain circumstances. While describing the decision as shameful, Bajto wasn't surprised. For him, the ruling was part of a long process of institutionalizing neofascism in the country. "Jews and Serbs don't feel safe here. That is a message that they're not important and their feelings aren't important. They [Jews, Serbs, and minorities] are worried about what comes next," he said.

Flipping through a stack of old newspapers, Bajto pointed to various front-page headlines criticizing Serbia's government, Serbian nationalism, and Serb war criminals from the Yugoslav wars. At twenty years old, *Novosti* has carved out a reputation as one of the few voices that defends the rights of minorities caught between competing strands of nationalism. But to Croatia's far right, *Novosti* was little more than a mouthpiece for the Serb minority. As Bajto explained, "Throughout the last five years, there is a revival of everything dark that happened in the nineties: fascist resurgence and ultraconservative organizations and agendas. . . . There was a period of liberal normalization after 2000, but now it's a revival again, a period of nationalistic purification of culture in Croatia." Bajto continued:

Now, for the first time in recent history, we have this official recognition of Croatian fascists from the Second World War through the council established by the prime minister. That is really something new, and it's a rewriting of history. And in the media, in culture, and everywhere on the internet, you have this equalization of anti-fascism of the Second World War with the Ustaše, who are now just considered Croatian patriots. Jasenovac is a myth, they try to say the number of people killed was lower, or the camp was a work camp and not the site of exterminations.

While the anti-fascist movement is embattled and marginalized, Bajto insists it is "not insignificant." With much of the country against them, anti-fascists continue to fight for the rights of ethnic minorities, the LGBTQI community, asylum seekers, and others targeted by the far right. But the situation is grim. "It's becoming harder to find people who admit that the situation is very bad. There is a silencing effect taking hold of the country."

Back in his friend's Zagreb flat, Lovro Krnić insisted that anti-fascists will continue to play their part in changing the mainstream discourse in Croatia. "People send us pictures of neo-Nazi graffiti, and major newspapers have started citing [Anti-Fascist Courier] as a credible source of information," he said. "This fight for the past is a fight for our future."

NOTES

1. Sven Milekic, "Croatia Parliament Backs Controversial WWII Commemoration," *Balkan Insight*, February 5, 2016, http://www.balkaninsight.com/en/article/croatian-parliament-endorses-again-ww2-bleiburg-commemoration-02-05-2016.

2. Sven Milekic, "Anti-fascist Monuments: Croatia's 'Unwanted Heritage,'" *Balkan Insight*, April 3, 2017, http://www.balkaninsight.com/en/article/anti-fascist-monuments-croatia-s-unwanted-heritage—03-31-2017.

3. Sven Milekic, "The Strange Case of Miro Barešić—Reflections on A Controversial Memorialisation in Croatia," *Erinnerungskulturen*, November 2, 2016, https://erinnerung.hypotheses.org/924.

4. Sven Milekic, "Untold Stories of Croatia's Wartime Forced Evictions," *Balkan Insight*, April 20, 2016, http://www.balkaninsight.com/en/article/untold-stories-of-croatia-s-wartime-forced-evictions-04-19-2016.

5. Patrick Strickland, "Croatia's 'Alt-Right': A Dangerous Group on the Margins," *Al Jazeera English*, March 17, 2018, https://www.aljazeera.com/news/2018/03/croatia-alt-dangerous-group-margins-180315120558413.html.

6. Sven Milekić, "Serbia Protests after Croatian Right-Wingers Burn Newspaper," *Balkan Insight*, September 4, 2017, http://www.balkaninsight.com/en/article/serbia-protests-weekly-burning-by-pro-ustasa—09-04-2017.

7. Sven Milekic, "Croatian Rightists Disrupt Anti-fascist Anniversary Rally," *Balkan Insight*, July 27, 2016, http://www.balkaninsight.com/en/article/rightist-try-to-stop-croatian-wwii-anti-fascist-anniversary-07-27-2016.

8. Sven Milekic, "Croatian Fascist Slogan Deemed Unconstitutional but Allowable," *Balkan Insight*, February 28, 2018, http://www.balkaninsight.com/en/article/croatian-fascist-slogan-deemed-unconstitutional-but-permitted-02-28-2018/1431/2.

SEARCHING FOR A SAFE PLACE

In March 2016, I met Ramadan, a forty-seven-year-old Syrian actor whose wife and children were still stuck in his native Homs. We sat in his small de facto room—two bunk beds cordoned off by cardboard walls—in Berlin's Prenzlauer Berg neighborhood. He recalled his torturous journey from a Syrian interrogation room to Germany.

He received his first interrogation summons in 2013, as protests and armed battles gripped much of Syria, particularly Homs. With family members in the Free Syrian Army, a loose-knit rebel group fighting the government since the conflict's outset, he knew his interrogators would spare him no mercy. "They were very tough on me," he told me. "There was no torture during the first week, but I had to walk over dead bodies to get to the toilet. Other detainees were sleeping in rooms next to dead bodies."

A squat, bareheaded man who gestures expressively with his hands as he speaks, Ramadan lowered his head and silently paused for several minutes while preparing himself to recall the second week of detention. "The second week was worse. At the beginning they just burned me with cigarettes. They would put their cigarettes out on me while interrogating me." As he cleared his throat to speak again, tears covered Ramadan's face, his voice shaking as he struggled to drag up memories he would have pre-

CONCLUSION

ferred to leave behind. Aware that he had worked on an Al Jazeera Arabic documentary in Homs before the uprising, the interrogators accused him of receiving funds from Qatar, the country that owns and funds the network. "They were asking me,
'Where's the money from Al Jazeera? Where is your laptop?
Where are the guns?'" "That's when the behavior was mon-
strous," he said, speaking of the beatings and torture. "They
wanted to take the last of my dignity. They cursed my wife, my
sisters, my daughters as they did it."

On the last day of interrogation, his captors kept up the ques-
tions and beatings from 7:30 a.m. until 2:30 the next morning. "I
was shocked because it was the first time I saw someone who is
only a person in appearance. Inside him there was no humanity.
He was a monster. I hate saying this, but for him all that mattered
was that I am Sunni." The next morning, one of his interrogators
woke Ramadan from his sleep and informed him that he had a
"present, a surprise" for him. "He told me, 'I see you here in interrogation, and then I go home and see you on the television.'
The only reason I've been easy on you is because my daughter
loves your shows.' Then, they took me to the judge at some place
and I was charged with not having completed military service."
He was released after paying a hefty fine and allowed to return
home, but his nights were sleepless, plagued by the memories
of torture, the images of lifeless cadavers on the jail cell floors.
For the next four months, Ramadan said, he was unable to go
outside, to speak to people normally. "I was just too scared to
leave home."

Ramadan supports the uprising against Syrian president Bashar al-Assad, though he has grown disillusioned and hopeless. For him and many others who have experienced the darkest elements of the Syrian regime's torture chambers, the dream of a free Syria has morphed into a nightmare.

As the years passed, the conflict grew more overtly sectarian, pitting the largely Sunni opposition against some members of minority communities who threw their weight behind the Assad government for fear of hardline Islamist armed groups. As opposition groups and the regime fought for territory, the latter responded with barrel bombs, chemical weapons, and killing on an industrial scale. Ramadan recalled a moment when regime forces stopped him and a fellow traveler at a checkpoint back in September 2015. "I thought, OK, it's over. Death is better than any more torture. Then I heard them speaking on the phone. I heard them speaking on the walkie-talkies and they mentioned the airport," he said, referring to a detention center known for its torture. "Whoever enters the airport dies. But after the negotiations and a bribe, they threw us in the middle of the desert near Palmyra."

The Syrian security officers accepted a bribe of two hundred thousand Syrian pounds (around U.S.$909). Ramadan and another detainee were left in the middle of the mine-blanketed desert outside of Palmyra with no choice but to walk through the dangerous terrain. The two men, neither of whom had any money left, feared that another police vehicle would pass by and pick them up. "There were mines everywhere," he recalled. "We knew if we waited there more *shabiha* [government forces] may come by. Should we die from mines or die from the regime? We decided to walk." Without water or food, the pair walked for hours until they reached a nearby village held by Syrian opposition forces. There, they camped for fifteen days until they decided it was safe enough to hire a smuggler and move on.

After the fifteen days in hiding, Ramadan and his companion set off for the Turkish border with the ultimate hope of reaching Europe and bringing their relatives there. Ramadan, however, first had to cross through Palmyra, then under the control of ISIL. "I had heard of ISIL before. I had heard of the Afghan fighters, the foreign fighters. They controlled Palmyra completely. I was surprised when I first saw them at the checkpoint—the way they looked, their beards, their clothes. You feel like you've gone back in time fifteen hundred years. You feel like you're in a film."

After passing through the city, they had to go through al-Nusra Front checkpoints. Making it through safely, Ramadan arrived at rebel checkpoints. That's when he broke down in tears. "They opened the door. They asked if any of us had cigarettes— I knew they were human. No one asked about my sect, if I'm Sunni or Alawite," he said, referring to different religious sects in Syria, the latter of which Assad belongs to. "They didn't care.... I felt that I came back from death." From there, Ramadan continued on his own, eventually arriving at the Turkish border. After waiting for several days, he was able to enter Turkey. He remained there for a few weeks while a smuggler organized his voyage to Europe. The smuggler let him know that his departure date from Turkey to the Greek island of Lesbos was October 10, 2015.

Ramadan was one of more than a million refugees and migrants who took boats and flimsy dinghies to European shores in 2015. Along with forty-seven others, most of whom were Syrian, he crossed the Aegean in an inflatable raft that he estimates was made for a maximum load of twenty-five people. "There were so many children on it. We went out in the night. The kids were crying. We kept telling them, 'See the light there in the distance? That's where we are going.'" Four hours later, they landed, the boat already halfway full of water and on the brink of sinking. They emerged onto the rocky shores and made their way back to solid land after, as Ramadan put it, seeing death yet again.

From there, Ramadan made the same journey that hundreds of thousands made before him, voyaging through mainland Greece and the Balkans until he reached Germany. Now in Berlin, he wavers between optimism, depression, and longing for his family, friends, and country. "I miss Syria," he said. "Some of the Germans treat us like savages. Can you imagine entering the bathroom and there are instructions on how to use the toilet? You feel ashamed. I had the same one in my house in Syria. I know how to use it. It makes me sad."

While many Europeans made world headlines when they rolled out the red carpet for refugees and migrants fleeing war and economic deprivation, the influx of arrivals also provided the hardline right with a renewed voice. "People coming from this war will act a certain way, so it's not just the fault of Germans. But we aren't animals." Ramadan, like hundreds of thousands of others, waited eagerly to find out if his family would be able to join him. In the meantime, he spent each day waiting for his wife to call, waiting for another temporary assurance that none of his relatives had died. News of humanitarian pauses in fighting or ceasefire negotiations did little to alleviate his pain. And in this aspect, the loneliness and fear, he is not alone. Ramadan is one of more than 4.8 million UN-registered Syrian refugees outside the country's borders. Millions more are internally displaced, either unable or unwilling to leave their homeland.

As the uprising continued, it drew the involvement of the United States, European countries, Russia, Turkey, Iran, and Gulf Arab regimes, as well as the Lebanese political party and armed group Hezbollah. Israel sporadically launches air strikes as well. With the United States, Turkey, and others executing their own bombing campaigns, it became clearer by the day that a growing number of countries felt the right to occupy a slice of Syria's skies and lands.

As is always the case with war, civilians pay the highest price. While the UN repeatedly urges Syrian parties to return to the negotiating table, the reality on the ground shows that the war in Syria is far from over. The need for people to find security in Europe and elsewhere is also far from over, but much of the world has stood by with folded arms, and Europe has sealed its gates. "Every person wants to go back to Syria, but if there is security," Ramadan said. "I lived freely in Syria before. Now I miss that. We aren't hungry for food here. We are still hungry for freedom."

For Ramadan, however, being separated from his family and navigating between antirefugee racism and Islamophobia are challenging. "You start to feel that your entire life exists in the cellphone, in WhatsApp, in Facebook. You feel it most at night when you come back to your room and lay in bed. You remember that you're by yourself. If you're happy, you're still alone. If you're sad, you're sad alone. I want my family in front of me, not on the other side of the line. When you put your phone in your pocket, you are putting your whole life in it."

Referring to the political climate in Germany and Europe at large, he said: "I can't go back to Syria, but I also feel that many people don't want us here. You don't know what it feels like to be treated like this, to be unwelcome." Ramadan's story is only one of millions like it, and many refugees and migrants who reached Europe have been targeted by far-right violence. At the time of writing, May 2018, the prospects remain grim. In Germany, the AfD is attempting to rewrite the country's hate speech laws, claiming that Germans are also victims of racism and incitement. "The AfD wants just one thing," said parliamentarian Jens Maier when presenting the bill to the parliament. "Namely that Germans are also protected from hate speech and mockery. Our draft bill is supposed to close a gap in the criminal code."[1]

In Austria, tens of thousands attended a commemoration for Croatian fascists and their relatives who were killed by Yugoslav Partisans at the tail end of the Second World War. The government, which was formed as a coalition of the right-wing Austrian People's Party and the far-right Austrian Freedom Party, refused to intervene.[2]

Unknown assailants smashed headstones in the Jewish section of the First Cemetery of Athens in early May 2018.[3] The incident was just the latest in a long string of anti-Semitic incidents in Greece. No one took credit for the vandalism, but far-right groups had claimed responsibility for similar acts in the past. Just over three months earlier, an assailant spray-painted "Golden Dawn" on a Holocaust memorial in Thessaloniki after a massive rally against negotiations between Athens and Skopje in a dispute over the name Macedonia.[4] That same day, Greek media outlets reported that anti-Semitic fliers were scattered on several streets in the city. They called Thessaloniki mayor Yiannis Boutaris a "slave of the Jews."[5]

On April 21, 2018, around one hundred far-right provocateurs from Generation Identity tried to erect a makeshift fence to prevent refugees and migrants from crossing the Alps into France. "Those who pay for it are the French," Romain Espino, a spokesperson for the group, told media.[6]

On April 22, bands of far-right attackers hurled Molotov cocktails, stones, and bottles at refugees in Lesbos, the Greek island that just two weeks earlier had been nominated for the Nobel Peace Prize for its heartwarming solidarity with asylum seekers.[7] "Burn them alive!" the assailants screamed as they carried out the assault.

In Germany, anti-Semitic attacks soared in 2017, with an average of four such incidents a day.[8] According to official figures breaking, 93 percent of incidents during the first eight months of the year "were linked to far-right extremism."[9]

In many countries, the state appeared keener to crack down on anti-fascists than to prevent the surge of xenophobia, hate, and far-right violence. For example, in Italy's Macerata, the site of a chilling neofascist shooting targeting six migrants just months earlier, police announced an investigation into a group of anti-fascists who hung up a piñata of dictator Benito Mussolini on April 24, the day marking the country's liberation from fascism.[10]

Despite the challenges—far-right parliamentary gains across the continent, an uptick in violence, and the bellicosity of state authorities—European anti-fascists like the ones I wrote about in this book are fighting back. Marcos, a Greek anti-fascist who spoke to me in May 2018 with a pseudonym, sat in the Notara squat in the Exarchia district of Athens. A stern-faced man with a rugged goatee, Marcos recalled a fascist attack two years earlier on the squat, home at the time to nearly one hundred refugees and migrants. Facing threats of violence and the ever-present possibility of police raids, Marcos insists the squatters and the migrant residents refuse to be intimidated. "All the people in this struggle are walking a path created by comrades before us," he said, arguing that anti-fascism is a strategy that demands ample planning, laborious work, and prescriptive politics predicated on changing society rather than merely resisting fascism. "Asking if we're anti-fascists is like asking if we're humans. This [Notara] is a safe haven for these people. . . . This is a process of creating. . . . It takes a lot of time [and] effort. That needs organization."

During a general assembly later that night, an activist led an Afghan refugee family into the squat's reception area. They were fatigued and searching for a place to stay. Their bags were weatherworn, their clothes disheveled, and their faces drained. From Afghanistan, the father, mother, and their two daughters made the journey by land and sea, crossing mountains, rivers, borders, and fields. With the help of a translator, Marcos explained the politics of Notara. The family said they understood and wanted to stay until they could find their own accommodation. Marcos flipped open a notebook and replied, "Let's see if we can find an open room for you."

NOTES

1. Ben Knight, "AfD Tries to Redefine German Hate Speech Laws," *Deutsche Welle*, April 27, 2018, http://www.dw.com/en/afd-tries-to-redefine-german-hate-speech-laws/a-43563462.

2. Patrick Strickland, "Thousands Attend Far-Right Commemoration in Southern Austria," *Al Jazeera English*, May 12, 2018, https://www.aljazeera.com/news/2018/05/thousands-attend-commemoration-southern-austria-180512164018335.html.

3. "Greek Jewish Body Deplores Desecration of Cemetery," *Ekathimerini*, May 7, 2018, http://www.ekathimerini.com/228388/article/ekathimerini/news/greek-jewish-body-deplores-desecration-of-cemetery.

4. "Vandalism of Holocaust Memorial in Thessaloniki condemned," *Ekathimerini*, January 23, 2018, http://www.ekathimerini.com/225166/article/ekathimerini/news/vandalism-of-holocaust-memorial-in-thessaloniki-condemned.

5. "Greek Jews Condemn Neo-Nazi Vandalism of Thessaloniki Holocaust Memorial," *Times of Israel*, January 25, 2018, https://www.timesofisrael.com/greek-jews-condemn-neo-nazi-vandalism-of-thessaloniki-holocaust-memorial/.

6. "Far-Right Activists Block Alps Pass Used by Migrants," *France 24*, April 21, 2018, http://www.france24.com/en/20180421-far-right-activists-genera tion-identityblock-alps-pass-used-migrants-col-Echelle.

7. Patrick Strickland, "Far-Right Attacks Increase Tension in Greece's Les-bos," *Al Jazeera English*, April 23, 2018, https://www.aljazeera.com/news/ 2018/04/attacks-increase-tension-greece-lesbos-180423103008546.html.

8. Derek Scally, "German Outrage over High-Profile Anti-Semitic Attacks," *Irish Times*, April 21, 2018, https://www.irishtimes.com/news/world/europe/ german-outrage-over-high-profile-anti-semitic-attacks-1.3468681.

9. Michelle Martin, "German Police Investigate Anti-Semitic Attack on Men in Berlin," Reuters, April 18, 2018, https://www.reuters.com/article/us-ger many-antisemitism/german-police-investigate-anti-semitic-attack-on-men-in-berlin-idUSKBN1HP23L.

10. Jessica Phelan, "Outcry after Italian Antifascists Hang a Mussolini Pi-ñata," *The Local*, April 27, 2018, https://www.thelocal.it/20180427/mussolini-pinata-macerata-italy.

CONCLUSION

INDEX

AK Press is small, in terms of staff and resources, but we also manage to be one of the world's most productive anarchist publishing houses. We publish close to twenty books every year, and distribute thousands of other titles published by like-minded independent presses and projects from around the globe. We're entirely worker run and democratically managed. We operate without a corporate structure—no boss, no managers, no bullshit.

The Friends of AK program is a way you can directly contribute to the continued existence of AK Press, and ensure that we're able to keep publishing books like this one! Friends pay $25 a month directly into our publishing account ($30 for Canada, $35 for international), and receive a copy of every book AK Press publishes for the duration of their membership! Friends also receive a discount on anything they order from our website or buy at a table: 50 percent on AK titles, and 20 percent on everything else. We have a Friends of AK e-book program as well: $15 a month gets you an electronic copy of every book we publish for the duration of your membership. You can even sponsor a deeply discounted membership for someone in prison.

E-mail friendsofak@akpress.org for more info, or visit the Friends of AK Press website: akpress.org/friends.html.

There are always great book projects in the works—so sign up now to become a Friend of AK Press, and let the presses roll!